Appreciation Course for Panchayat Accountants

Appreciation Course for Panchayat Accountants

Institute of Public Auditors of India

GYAN

ipai

Published by

Gyan Publishing House
5, Ansari Road
Daryaganj, New Delhi-110002
Phone: 011-47034999, 9811692060
E-mail: books@gyanbooks.com

and

Institute of Public Auditors of India
223, 2nd Floor, 'C' Wing, AGCR Building,
I.P. Estate, New Delhi-110002
Ph.: 91-011-23702330, 23702290, 23702369
E-mail: ipai.hq@gmail.com,
Website: www.ipaiindia.org

Distribution Network
gyanbooks.com
India, USA, Canada, UK, Australia, France

ISBN: 978-93-6780-034-8 (HB)

First Published, 2024

Printed at: Gyan Press, Delhi.

Appreciation Course for Panchayat Accountants
Institute of Public Auditors of India

Contents

Preface

This handbook has been designed to support potential accountants, administrators and other stakeholders who may be interested in understanding Panchayati Raj Institutions accounting and financial management. The candidates appearing for the Panchayat Accountant Examination that is sought to be conducted by the Institute of Chartered Accountants of India in collaboration with and under the aegis of the Comptroller and Auditor General of India would also be greatly benefitted by this handbook.

The Constitution (seventy-third) Amendment Act, 1992 accorded the Panchayati Raj Institutions (PRIs) a constitutional status. Consequently, the States have established a system of three-tiers of PRIs viz. Gram Panchayat (GP) at the village level, Panchayat Samitis (PS) at the Block level and Zila Parishad (ZP) at the district level to enable them to function as institutions of local self-government.

To ensure that the vast financial resources made available to the Panchayats are properly utilised for the intended purposes, the Ministry of Panchayati Raj Institutions took up a project and signed a Memorandum of Understanding in 2016 with the Institute of Public Auditors of India to facilitate and assist the State Governments and Panchayats in proper preparation of budget, accounting of various transactions as well as auditing of accounts following the State specific procedures and guidelines and in line with the Model Accounting System advocated by the office of the Comptroller & Auditor General of India.

The Central and State governments are taking steps for capacity building and empowerment of PRIs to enable them to shoulder greater responsibilities arising from devolution of powers. It is, therefore, important that the elected representatives of people appreciate the role and responsibility of Panchayat Accountants and support them in effective discharge of their duties. They should have appreciation of the issues and concerns which relate to managing the Accounting System in an effective and efficient manner and mitigate risks of frauds and irregularities.

The essential features of PRIs, form of accounts, methodology to classify the transactions in accounts and accounting are quite unique. Finance Commissions have also given various recommendations in favour of PRIs. Over the years, the Ministry of Panchayat Raj and PRIs – the administrative ministry for PRIs has developed E-Gramswaraj Portal to capture transactions across receipt and expenditure.

Keeping in view the problems faced by the PRI Accountants at the Gram Panchayat, Block Level and Zila Parishad levels in the maintenance of accounts and special requirements of accounting to be adopted by the PRIs, the Institute of Public Auditors of India has developed this basic course material compiled in the form of a handbook suitable not only for the persons aspiring to become Panchayat Accountants but also those working as Panchayat Accountants.

This handbook explains in simple language: (i) The structure, functioning and powers of PRIs with reference to constitutional provisions and essential recommendations of the Finance Commissions, (ii) System and Form of accounts to be adopted by PRIs, as per the provisions of the Constitution of India, meaning of Consolidated Fund, Contingency Fund and Public Account, Voted/Charged expenditure, (iii) Methodology to be adopted for classification of transactions, Codification of heads of accounts and (iv) PRI accounts, Books, Accounting records and statements forming parts of accounts. The course structure also gives a brief introduction to E-Gramswaraj – digital platform used as accounting application along with various formats of MIS reports. These have been presented in a handbook.

This elementary guide will provide the readers with evolution, various recommendations of Finance Commissions relating to PRIs, salient features of the 73rd Constitutional Amendment Act, functions of Gram Panchayats and other details for the polity and governance.

Elected representatives of the Panchayats have the responsibility to manage the resources of Panchayats with compliance with various applicable laws, rules, regulations and accounting standards. The Panchayat Accountants play an important role in this mission.

We also hope that the elected representatives of people and functionaries at different levels concerned with governance of PRIs would find this handbook useful for training and awareness purposes.

The project is the result of desk research supplemented with field visits to see the practice being followed at the village, block and district levels.

I wish to place on record my sincere appreciation of the mentorship provided to the project by Ms. Shubha Kumar, former Dy. CAG and Vice President, IPAI. This handbook has taken shape under the meticulous guidance of Mrs Meenakshi Sharma, former Dy. CAG now holding the IPAI Chair in the Delhi School of Public Policy and Governance. She has been ably assisted by S/Shri V. K. Chandhok (New Delhi); R.B. Vyas, S.G. Tewani and K. J. Vaishnav (Ahmedabad); Ashwini Kumar Mishra, G.C. Sahoo and S.K. Gajendra (Bhubaneswar) and T.L. Sharma (Bhopal), all esteemed members of IPAI from IPAI Hqrs and the Gujarat, Madhya Pradesh and Odisha Chapters of IPAI.

Subhash Chandra Pandey
President
Institute of Public Auditors of India

Chapter - 1

Panchayati Raj Institutions – Structure and Functioning

1. INTRODUCTION

The Constitution (seventy-third) Amendment Act, 1992 accorded the Panchayati Raj Institutions (PRIs) a constitutional status. The main features of this important amendment are:

1. Establishment of Gram Sabha at village level comprising persons registered in the electoral rolls relating to a village within the area of Panchayat. (Article 243B)
2. Constitution of a three tier structure of Panchayats in every State and UTs – at village, intermediate and district level. (Article 243 B)
3. Reservation of seats for Scheduled Caste, Scheduled Tribes and Women. (Article 243 D)
4. Fixed tenure for Panchayat bodies. (Article 243 E)
5. Transfer of powers, authority and responsibilities to Panchayats, including 29 subjects listed in the Eleventh Schedule. (Article 243 G)
6. Powers to impose taxes. (Article 243 H)
7. Constitution of a Finance Commission to review finances of the Panchayats, recommend principles for appropriation of taxes, and to provide for grants-in-aids.
8. Audit of the accounts of PRIs.

9. Constitution of State Election Commission to supervise, direct and control smooth elections to Panchayat bodies.

The State profile of PRIs differ from State to State depending upon the total geographical area of the State viz-à-viz rural population in the respective State.

2. WHAT ARE THE PANCHAYATI RAJ INSTITUTIONS (PRIS)

Following the enactment of the 73rd Amendment Act, the States have established a system of three-tiers of PRIs viz. Gram Panchayat (GP) at the village level, Panchayat Samitis (PS) at the Block level and Zila Parishad (ZPs) at the district level to enable them to function as institutions of self-Government level. Some States have two-tier Panchayats- at village level and at district level. The three tiers of PRIs are:

- Gram Panchayats – village level
- Block Panchayats – intermediary level
- Zila Panchayats – district level

(1) Gram (Village) Panchayats (GP)

Gram Panchayat is the first tier of PRIs at the village level. At the rural level, the GP constitutes the foundation of the PRI system. Generally, every Gram Panchayat shall consist of elected Panches and a Sarpanch. The Sarpanch is elected as per the provisions in the respective State Act. The Sarpanch shall be responsible for carrying out the activities and resolutions of the GP, all directions issued by the State Government and all functions assigned to the GP as per the Act of a State. He would be responsible to ensure proper maintenance of records and registers, authorise payments, issue of cheque and refunds, etc.

Further, the State Acts also provide that the State Government or the prescribed authority may appoint a Secretary for a Gram Panchayat or group of two or more Gram Panchayats. It is the duty of the Secretary of the GP to convene and record the proceedings of meetings of Gram Sabha and GP, regulate the functioning of GP, maintain all the official records in GP, prepare annual plan of GP, prepare estimates of revenue and expenditure and recover taxes and other dues of GP. The Secretary is also responsible for maintaining cleanliness and hygiene, maintenance and upkeep of water resources, lighting and construction of village roads, promotion of youth welfare, implementation of programmes for social welfare and any other activities entrusted by the State Government, ZP or BP.

(2) Taluka (Block) Panchayats (BP)

The Block Panchayats (BPs) are the intermediate tier of PRIs at the Block level. These consist of members elected from the constituencies, who are empowered to elect a President and a Vice-President. The President shall be responsible for carrying out the activities and resolution of the BP, all directions issued by the State Government and all functions assigned to the BP as per the provisions of the respective Act in the State Government. He would be responsible to ensure proper maintenance of records and registers, authorise payments, issue of cheque and refunds, etc.

Further, generally the State Government shall appoint for every BP a Chief Executive Officer (CEO) as the administrative head and may also appoint one or more Additional Chief Executive Officers, who shall discharge such functions and perform such duties as may be assigned to them by the CEO. The CEO, BP shall be assisted by a number of officers, (i.e. BDO, Accounts Officer, technical staff like Assistant Engineers and other administrative staff. CEO, BP shall be responsible to take action for implementation of resolution of ZP, supervise and control the execution of all activities of BP. He is authorised to draw and disburse money out of the ZP fund as per the financial rules in this regard.

(3) Zila (District) Panchayats (ZP)

Zila Panchayats (ZPs) are the third and topmost tier of Panchayats at the district level. In every district there is a ZP. Every ZP shall consist of members elected from the constituencies, who are empowered to elect a President, etc. The President shall be responsible for carrying out the activities of resolution of the ZP, all directions issued by the State Government and all functions assigned to the ZP. He would be responsible to ensure proper maintenance of records and registers, authorise payments, issue of cheque and refunds, etc. Further, the State Government shall appoint for every ZP a Chief Executive Officer (CEO) and may also appoint one or more Additional Chief Executive Officers, who shall discharge such functions and perform such duties as may be assigned to them by the CEO. The CEO is the administrative head and assisted by Departments like Public Health, Public Works, Rural Engineering, etc. CEO, ZP shall also be responsible to take action for resolutions of ZP, supervise and control the execution of all activities of ZP. He is authorised to draw and disburse money out of the ZP fund as per the financial rules in this regard.

The CEO, ZP is responsible for preparing the budget for the planned development of the district and utilisation of the resources, drawing up annual plans for the economic development of the district and social justice and ensuring their implementation. CEO, ZP is also responsible for coordination, evaluation and monitoring of the schemes entrusted by the Central or State Government, appropriation of the grants received from the Central or State Government to the second tier of Panchayats (Block Panchayat) and GPs in accordance with the specified criteria.

3. FUNCTIONING OF PRIs

According to the provisions of **Article 243 G** of the Constitution, the Legislature of a State may, by law, endow the Panchayats with such powers and authority as may be necessary to enable them to function as institutions of self-government and such law may contain provision for the devolution of powers and responsibility upon Panchayats at the appropriate level, subject to such conditions as may be specified therein, with respect to:

(a) The preparation of plans for economic development and social justice;

(b) The implementation of schemes for economic development and social justice as may be entrusted to them including those in relation to the matters listed in the Eleventh Schedule.

Similarly, according to the provisions of **Article 243 H** of the Constitution, the legislature of state may:

(a) Authorise a Panchayat to levy, collect and appropriate such taxes, duties, tolls and fees in accordance with such procedure and subject to such limits,

(b) Assign to a Panchayat such taxes, duties, tolls and fees levied and collected by the State Government for such purposes and subject to such conditions and limits,

(c) Provide for making such Grants-in-Aid to the Panchayats from the Consolidated Fund of the State and

(d) Provide for the constitution of such funds for crediting all moneys received, by or on behalf of the Panchayats and also for the withdrawal of such money there from as may be specified in the Law.

3.1 Given the above backdrop, broadly the functions of three-tier panchayat structure are generally as follows:

Gram panchayat

- Drinking water facilities for domestic use and for animals.
- Scavenging of roads in the villages.
- Maintenance of community properties.
- Lighting arrangement in villages.
- Spread of education including primary education in villages.
- Planning of rural development.
- Supervision of crops in the outskirt of village.
- Planning for agricultural improvements.
- Planning for Agricultural Reforms.

Taluka/ Block Panchayat

- Provide health and hygiene services in talukas.
- Control on epidemics.
- Constructions and maintenance of village roads.
- Establishment and management of primary schools.
- Agricultural improvements and planning at taluka level.
- Women welfare, development of youth activities and assistance.
- Help in natural and manmade disasters like flood, fire accidents, etc.

District/ Zilla Panchayat

- Out of the 29 functions, major functions are transferred to the District / Zilla Panchayats subject to transfer of funds by the Line departments of the State Government for execution of the programmes of the ZPs itself.
- Control over activities of district panchayats, taluka panchayats and gram panchayats.
- To provide assistance.
- Management and control on activities transferred from Revenue, Education, Co-operation, Irrigation, Agriculture by State Govt.
- Monitoring of activities of Panchayats Department at district level.

4. DEVOLUTION OF FUNCTIONS, FUNDS TO PRIs

The 73rd Constitutional Amendment envisages that all the 29 subjects as listed in Eleventh Schedule of the Constitution along with funds and functionaries would be eventually transferred to the PRIs through suitable legislation of the State Government. List of the 29 subjects is at **Annexure-I.** Accordingly, most of the departments of the respective States have transferred their respective functions to the PRIs in the States. The PRIs are now authorised to impose taxes on holdings, professions and levy tolls, fees and rates.

4.1 Sources of Funds

1. PRIs receive funds from Central Government (Central Finance Commission grants, Scheme funds), State Government (State finance commission grants, scheme funds, other grants-in-aid, assigned revenue).
2. They also generate their own revenues from; Land Revenue, Vehicle Tax, Tax on industries, Toll Tax, Festival, Melas and Fairs Tax, House Tax, Entertainment Tax, Licence Fees, Cattle Registration Tax, Water Rates, Public Lighting Tax, etc.
3. State legislature may, authorise and assign to a Panchayat to levy, collect and appropriate taxes, duties, tolls and fees.
4. Provide for establishment of funds for crediting all money received by or on behalf of the Panchayats and also for the withdrawal of such money therefrom.
5. The PRIs may take loans from the NGOs, Trusts and International Agencies.
6. PRIs may keep funds in treasury or in the accredited bank account as per directions of the State Government for funds received from State Government and in bank accounts for funds received under Central Schemes, Central Finance Commission grants as well as from their own sources of revenue.

5. ACCOUNTS, AUDIT, SUPERVISION AND GUIDANCE OF PRIs

In order to strengthen the process of accounts, audit, supervision and guidance of PRIs, the Finance Commissions in its reports have given observations / recommendations. The Finance Commission(s) have been particular about the role and responsibility of the C&AG in matters of control and supervision over the proper maintenance of accounts and audit for all the tiers / levels of panchayats. The FC also recommended for CAG to be entrusted with the Technical Guidance and Support (TGS) over the audit of all the local bodies at every tier / category and his Annual Technical Inspection Report (ATIR) as well as Annual Report of Director of Local Fund Audit (DLFA) must be placed before the State Legislature. Some of the important observations / recommendations of Finance Commissions are given hereunder:

Summary of Important Observations / Recommendations of *Finance Commissions. Eleventh Finance Commission*

(a) States should review the existing accounting heads under which funds are being transferred to the local bodies. For each such major head/sub-major head, six minor heads should be created - three for the PRIs and another three for the ULBs - so that a clear picture of transfers to each category of local bodies is readily available. This may be done in consultation with the C&AG and the Controller General of Accounts, to ensure uniformity among the States.

(b) The C&AG should be entrusted with the responsibility of exercising control and supervision over the proper maintenance of accounts and their audit for all the tiers/levels of panchayats and urban local bodies.

(c) The Director, Local Fund Audit or any other agency made responsible for the audit of accounts of the local bodies, should work under the technical and administrative supervision of the C&AG.

(d) The C&AG should prescribe the format for the preparation of budgets and for keeping of accounts for the local bodies. Such formats should be amenable to computerisation in a networked environment.

(e) Local bodies particularly the village level panchayats and in some cases the intermediate level panchayats, that do not have trained accounts staff, may contract out the upkeep of accounts to outside agencies/persons. For this purpose:

   (i) The C&AG may lay down the qualifications and experience for the agency/person who could be contracted out the work of maintenance of accounts. The Director, Local Fund Audit or his equivalent authority may do the registration of such agency/person.

(ii) A group of local bodies may be entrusted to an agency/ person for upkeep of accounts on payment of remuneration as may be fixed by the C&AG in consultation with the State Government.

(iii) The Director, Local Fund Audit or his equivalent authority, under the direction of the C&AG, may do the supervision over the quality of work of such agency/person.

(iv) Non-compliance or poor performance should lead to deregistration of the agency/person entrusted with such task.

(f) The report of the C&AG relating to audit of accounts of the panchayats and the municipalities should be placed before a Committee of the State Legislature constituted on the same lines as the Public Accounts Committee.

Technical Guidance and Supervision

As per the FC-XI report, the Technical Guidance and Supervision (TG&S) of maintenance of accounts and audit was to be entrusted to the C&AG. The components of TG&S include:

(i) setting audit standards and audit planning;

(ii) adoption of improved audit methodologies;

(iii) training in audit and accounts and

(iv) annual transactions audit by random selection and supplementary audit of institutions audited by the State Director of Local Fund Audit.

Twelfth Finance Commission

PRIs and ULBs should, out of the grants allocated, give high priority to expenditure on creation of data base and maintenance of accounts through the use of modern technology and management systems, wherever possible. Some of the modern methods like GIS for mapping of properties in urban areas and computerization for switching over to a modern system of financial management would go a long way in creating strong local governments.

Thirteenth Finance Commission

The C&AG should issue directions for classification of revenue receipts of the states providing details of duties, tolls and fees collected so that the SFCs can make appropriate recommendations.

It is necessary that the C&AG be entrusted with TG&S for all local bodies for all states. This will also be a necessary consequence of the standardisation of accounting formats for all local bodies across states. Further, the Annual Technical Inspection Report of the C&AG as well as the Annual Report of the Director of Local Fund Audit should be placed before the state legislature.

The finance accounts should include a separate statement indicating head-wise details of actual expenditures under the same heads as used in the budget for both Panchayati Raj Institutions (PRIs) and Urban Local Bodies (ULBs).

Fourteenth Finance Commission

The local bodies should be required to spend the grants only on the basic services within the functions assigned to them under relevant legislations.

The books of accounts prepared by the local bodies should distinctly capture income on account of own taxes and non-taxes, assigned taxes, devolution and grants from the State, grants from the Finance Commission and grants for any agency functions assigned by the Union and State Governments. The technical guidance and support arrangements by the C&AG should be continued and the States should take action to facilitate local bodies to compile accounts and have them audited in time.

Fifteenth Finance Commission

Accounts and Audit

Integration of the Financial Management Systems

The timely availability of audited accounts separately at the local body level and jointly at the State and all-India level – continues to be a problem despite the emphasis laid by previous Commissions. We consider the availability of accounts online, both before and after audit, of all three levels of government a critical reform agenda.

The upgraded PRIAsoft software needs to be integrated with the Integrated Financial Management Information System (IFMIS) of the State Governments (wherever it exists) and the Public Financial Management System (PFMS) of the CGA in the Union Government in order to generate online accounts by each rural local body, enable online auditing of such accounts and their consolidation at the State and all-India levels.

To achieve this objective, the report suggested a two-stage process. First, the integration of the PRIASoft and NMAM systems with the State-level IFMIS and, subsequently, with PFMS to achieve complete integration. It recommended that under the guidance of the CAG, the concerned ministries and CGA shall develop, on a trial basis, an integrated account maintenance system as stated above for the States before 31 March 2021, ready for full roll-out from 1 April 2021.

SUM-UP

1. The Constitution 73rd Amendment Act 1992 brought out the concept of PRIs. The 73rd Amendment envisages transfer of functions / funds to PRIs.
2. A three-tier system of Panchayat Raj Institutions viz. (a) Zila Panchayat; (b) Block Panchayat; and (c) Gram Panchayat had been established by the Governments.
3. Gram Panchayat ensures execution of schemes and work assigned by Central or State Government or Zila/ Block Panchayat.
4. Block Panchayat execute, supervise and monitor schemes and works through Gram Panchayat or Executing Agency.
5. Zila Panchayat coordinate, evaluate, monitor and guide the Block and Gram Panchayat.
6. As per Article 243G of the Constitution, the Legislature of a State may endow the Panchayats with powers and authority to enable them to function as a local self-government, to prepare plan for economic development and implementation of schemes.
7. As per Article 243H of the Constitution, the Legislature of a State may authorise a Panchayat to levy, collect and appropriate taxes etc. and assign to a Panchayat such taxes, duties levied / collected by State Government, make grants, provide for constitution of funds for crediting of moneys received etc.
8. The Gram Panchayats / Block Panchayats and Zila Panchayats have different welfare functions towards society and the ZPs are tasked with monitoring, control and management / supervision of activities under GPs / BPs / ZPs.

9. PRIs: (i) have funds from Centre / State Govts / Central Finance Commission, (ii) impose taxes, (iii) can raise loans and (iv) may keep funds in treasury / bank.

10. Different Finance Commissions have been particular about the role, responsibility of C&AG in matters of control and supervision over proper maintenance of accounts and audit for all tiers of Panchayats.

11. The Finance Commission also recommended for CAG to be entrusted with Technical, Guidance and Supervision over the auditing of all local bodies. The TGS envisaged: (i) setting audit standards and audit planning; (ii) adoption of improved audit methodologies; (iii) training in audit and accounts and use of technology / computerisation, integration of financial management system.

Chapter - 2

Form of Government Accounts

2.1 INTRODUCTION

The form of accounts of the Union, States and Union Territory governments have been devised keeping in view the provisions of various articles of the Constitution and sections of Union Territories Act, 1963. According to Article 150 of Constitution, the form in which the accounts of the Union and of States shall be kept are to be prescribed by the President on the advice of the Comptroller and Auditor General of India. These provisions ensure the uniformity in the structure of accounts of the Government of India and the State Governments. The responsibility for prescribing the form of accounts, and to frame, or revise, rules and manuals relating thereto on behalf of the President of India in terms of Article 150 of the Constitution of India on the advice of the Comptroller and Auditor General of India lies with the Controller General of Accounts. The duties and powers of the Comptroller and Auditor General of India are contained in the Comptroller and Auditor General's (Duties, Powers and Conditions of Service) Act of 1971. In this chapter we will learn about the form of government accounts and the concepts of charged and voted expenditure. This would help us in appreciating how public funds are kept and accounted for.

2.2 MAIN DIVISIONS OF ACCOUNTS

The government accounts are kept in three parts :

1. Consolidated Fund
2. Contingency Fund
3. Public Account

There being no separate Public Account in the case of Union Territory Governments, the transactions pertaining to this account are recorded in the Public Account of the Central Government.

2.2.1 Consolidated Fund

In the **Consolidated Fund** there are two main parts namely; (1) Revenue and (2) Capital.

Revenue consists of

- 'Receipt heads (Revenue Account) - dealing with the proceeds of taxation and other receipts classed as revenue.
- 'Expenditure heads (Revenue Account)- dealing with expenditure met therefrom.

The second part (Capital) comprises the following sections:

- 'Receipt heads (Capital Account)'- dealing with receipts of capital nature which cannot be applied as a set off to capital expenditure.
- 'Expenditure heads (Capital Account)'- dealing with expenditure usually from borrowed funds with the objective of increasing assets of permanent character. It also includes receipts of a capital nature intended to be applied as set off to capital expenditure.
- Public Debt, Loans and Advances which comprise loans raised and their repayments by Government such as Internal Debt, External Debt of the Central Government, and Loans and Advances made by Government and their recoveries transactions relating to 'Appropriation to Contingency Fund' and Inter-State Settlement.

Under Article 266 (1) of The Constitution of India, all revenues received by the Government of India, all loans raised by it and also the recoveries of loans granted by it form the Consolidated Fund of India. Similarly, all revenues received by the Government of a State, all loans raised by it and also moneys received by it in repayment of loans granted by it form the Consolidated Fund of the State.

No expenditure can be incurred from the Consolidated Fund and no money can be withdrawn from the fund without authorisation from the Parliament/ State Legislature.

As stated earlier, the Consolidated Fund consists of revenue account and capital account. The 'Revenue Account' deals with the proceeds of taxation and other revenue receipts (such as Income Tax, Corporation Tax, Central Excise and Service Tax) and the expenditure met therefrom. The 'Capital Account' deals with expenditure met from borrowed funds with the objects of either increasing concrete assets of durable nature or reducing the recurring liabilities. It also includes capital receipts, so far as they relate to expenditure previously debited to capital head of expenditure, accruing during the process of construction of a project and utilised in reduction of capital expenditure. It may be noted that though the capital expenditure is usually met from borrowed funds and other resources outside the revenue account, there is no bar to meet capital expenditure from ordinary revenues, provided there is sufficient revenue to cover this expenditure. The 'Capital Account' also covers: (i) loans raised by Government and their repayments, and (ii) loans and advances paid by the Government and their recoveries. This also includes certain special types of heads/transactions relating to the Contingency Fund and inter-state suspense.

2.2.2 Contingency Fund

In **Contingency Fund** of the accounts, the transactions connected with the Contingency Fund set up by the Government of India or by a State or a Union Territory Government under Article 267 of Constitution/ Sector 48 of the Union Territories Act 1963, are recorded.

This Fund is established by law, by Parliament or by State Legislature of a State into which shall be paid from time to time such sums as may be determined by such law, and the said fund shall be placed at the disposal of the President or the Governor of a State, as the case may be, to enable advance to be made by him out of such fund for the purposes of meeting unforeseen expenditure pending authorisation of such expenditure by the Parliament or the State Legislature by Law. The Contingency Fund is in the nature of an imprest.

The corpus of the 'Contingency Fund' is created by debit to the Consolidated Fund of India or of the State. When expenditure is incurred out of an advance from the Contingency Fund, the expenditure is entered under the same head under the 'Contingency Fund' under which it would have been booked had the expenditure been incurred from the Consolidated Fund concerned. When such advance is paid from the 'Contingency Fund', the corpus of the Fund gets depleted. Subsequently, with the regularisation of the expenditure by obtaining vote of Parliament / State Legislature, the amount of advance is recouped to the corpus of the Contingency Fund by debit to the Consolidated Fund of the Union/

State. The expenditure is then entered under the same head under the Consolidated Fund, as revenue or capital expenditure, as the case may be. The adjustments in accounts for recoupment of Contingency Fund are required to be done in the same year in which Appropriation Act is passed. Where this is not done it may result in an adverse balance in the corpus of the Contingency Fund.

2.2.3 Public Account

In **Public Account** of the accounts, the transactions relating to Debt (other than those included in Consolidated Fund), 'Deposits', 'Advances', 'Remittances' and 'Suspense' are recorded. The transactions under Debt, Deposit and Advances in this part are such in respect of which Government incurs a liability to repay the money received or has a claim to recover the amounts paid, together with the repayments of the former (Debt and Deposits) and the recoveries of the latter (Advances). The transactions relating to 'Remittances' and 'Suspense' in this Part embrace all adjusting heads under which appear such transactions as remittances of cash between treasuries and currency chests and transfer between different accounting circles. The initial debts or credits to these heads are cleared eventually by corresponding receipts or payments either within the same circle of account or in another account circle.

All public moneys received by, or on behalf of, the Government of India or the Government of a State are credited to the Public Account of India or the Public Account of the Sate, as the case may be, as provided in Article 266(2) of the Constitution of India. However, this does not apply to: (i) all revenues received by the government, (ii) all loans raised by the government by the issue of treasury bills, (iii) ways and means advances and (iv) all moneys received in repayment of loans.

Any money, which is not to go to the Consolidated Fund, will be credited to Public Account. For payments out of this account, approval of the Parliament or the State Legislature is not required. The transactions relating to Remittances and Suspense are recorded in the Public Account only for a temporary period until these are transferred to appropriate accounts in the Consolidated Fund or the Public Account.

2.3 CONCEPTS OF CHARGED EXPENDITURE AND VOTED EXPENDITURE

Depending on the fact as to whether the expenditure is subject to vote of the legislature, the government expenditure is divided into: (1) charged expenditure and (2) voted expenditure. The details of these two forms of expenditure are given below:-

2.3.1 Charged Expenditure

(i) The Constitution provides for certain items of expenditure which, though form part of the annual budget, are not in the nature of demands for grants and are not put to the vote of the legislature. Such expenditure is called "Non voted" or "charged expenditure". These items of expenditure are of a fixed and inevitable nature and admit no variation (cannot be reduced or increased during discussion by the legislature),

(ii) The following items of expenditure shall be charged on the Consolidated Fund of India/State:

(a) The emoluments and allowances of the President/Governor and other items of expenditure relating to his office.

(b) The salaries and allowances of Chairman (Vice-President) and Deputy Chairman of Rajya Sabha and the Speaker and the Deputy Speaker of Lok Sabha. Similarly, those of the Speaker and Deputy Speaker of the Legislative Assemble and in the case of a State having Legislative Council also of the Chairman and the Deputy Chairman of the Legislative Council.

(c) The salaries, allowance and pensions payable to, or in respect of, Judges of the Supreme Court/ the High Courts. Administrative expenses of the Supreme Court/High Courts including all salaries, allowance and pension payable to or in respect of the officers and servants of the court concerned.

(d) The debt charges for which the Govt. of India/State is liable including interest, sinking fund charges, redemption charges and other expenditure relating to the raising of loans and service and redemption of debt.

(e) The salaries, allowances and pension payable to, or in respect of, the Comptroller and Auditor General of India as well as administrative expenses of the office of the Comptroller and Auditor General including all salaries, allowances and pensions payable to or in respect of persons serving in that office.

(f) the expenses of the Union Public Service Commission and State Public Service Commissions including salaries, allowances or pensions payable to or in respect of the members or staff of commissions.

(g) any sum required to satisfy judgment, decree award by any court or arbitral tribunal.

(h) any other items of expenditure declared by the Constitution or by Parliament/ State Legislature by law to be so charged.

(iii) It is open to either House of Parliament/State Legislature to discuss estimates relating in these items of expenditure, but they will not be submitted to vote by either Houses.

2.3.2 Voted Expenditure

The voted expenditure means expenditure of a general nature which is subject to vote of legislature. The legislature has full control on such expenditure, and it may be voted as included in the demands for grants, or after by imposing financial cuts here and there. Such expenditure can also be refused and, therefore, cannot be incurred without the vote and the approval of the legislature.

Any items of expenditure, which is 'voted', may be converted into the 'Charged' category by the law of the Parliament/ the State Legislature under the provision of Art 112(3)(g) of the Constitution. As a Bill intended to declare any expenditure 'Charged' upon the Consolidated Fund of India/State, falls under a category of Money Bill vide Art. 110 it is essential that all the conditions attached to a Money Bill are fulfilled and Bill passes through all the stages of legislation meant for a Money Bill.

Sum - Up

1. The government accounts are kept in three forms viz., Consolidated Fund, Contingency Fund and Public Account.
2. Under Article 266 (1) of the Constitution of India, all revenues received by the Government of India, all loans raised by it and also the recoveries of loans granted by it form part of the Consolidated Fund of India. Similarly, all revenues received by the Government of a State, all loans raised by it and also moneys received by it in repayment of loans granted by it form part of the Consolidated Fund of the State and no money can be withdrawn

from the Fund. All expenditure is incurred from the Consolidated Fund and no money can be withdrawn from the Fund without authorisation from the Parliament/ State Legislature.

3. The Consolidated Fund consists of revenue account and capital account. The 'Revenue Account' deals with the proceeds of taxation and other revenue receipts and the expenditure met therefrom. The 'Capital Account' deals with expenditure met from borrowed funds and other resources outside the revenue account. It also includes capital receipts.

4. Under Article 267 of the Constitution of India a 'Contingency Fund' may he established by law, by parliament or by State Legislature of a State into which shall be paid from time to time such sums as may be determined by law, and the said fund shall be placed at the disposal of the President or the Governor of a State, as the case may be, to enable advances to be made by him out of such fund for the purposes of meeting unforeseen expenditure pending authorisation of such expenditure by Parliament or the State Legislature by law.

5. All public moneys received by, or on behalf of the Government of India or the Government of a State are credited to the Public Account of India or the Public Account of the State, as the case may be, as provided in Article 266(2) of the Constitution of India except all revenues received by the government, all loans raised by the government by the issue of treasury bills, ways and means advances and all moneys received in repayment of loans. All transactions relating to debt (other than those included in the Consolidated Fund), deposits, advances, remittances and suspense are recorded in Public Accounts.

6. The Constitution provides for certain items of expenditure which though form part of the annual budget, are not in the nature of demands for grants and are not put to the vote of legislature. Such expenditure is called "charged expenditure". These items of expenditure are of a fixed and inevitable nature and cannot be reduced or increased during discussion by the legislature.

7. The expenditure of a general nature which is subject to vote of legislature is called "voted expenditure". The legislature has full control on such expenditure, and it may be voted as included in the demands for grants, or after imposing financial cuts here and there. Such expenditure can also be refused.

Chapter - 3

Classification of Transactions

3.1 INTRODUCTION

In Chapter 2, we have learnt about the forms of accounts and the concepts of capital/revenue, and charged/voted expenditures. Before learning about the accounting records of PRIs, it is necessary to become acquainted with the various heads of accounts and their codifications. In this chapter, we will learn about the constitutional provisions relating to the maintenance of accounts and need for classification of transactions, and the unit of classification including codification of various heads of accounts.

3.2 CONSTITUTIONAL PROVISIONS

Under Article 243J of the Constitution inserted vide Constitution (73rd Amendment) Act, 1992, the Legislature of the State may, by law, make provisions with respect to the maintenance of accounts by panchayats. The prescription would mean not only the broad form in which accounts would be kept but also the basis for selecting appropriate heads of accounts under which the transactions are to be classified. The heads of accounts shall be opened in conformity with these rules and in case of divergence, the receipt or expenditure shall be brought to account as determined by the State Government in consultation with the State Accountant General (A&E).

The State Governments did not have a uniform pattern in State Panchayat Rules for the maintenance of accounts. On the recommendations of the Eleventh Finance Commission (EFC) duly accepted by the Government of India, Comptroller and Auditor General of India devised formats for the budget and the accounts for Panchayati Raj Institutions

(PRIs) in October 2002. There is a general consensus on the acceptability of these formats among the States and many States have issued formal orders for their adoption.

The 73rd Amendment in Schedule XI of the Constitution enlarged the functional and financial domain of the PRIs. With the growth and diversity in the functions of PRIs and the need to accommodate transactions related to social and developmental activities, Panchayat operations have been presented in terms of functions, programmes, activities and the objects of expenditure. The structure constitutes a minute elaboration with which transactions are differentiated and classified. The multiple classifications bring together data in variety of ways for internal as well as external control for reporting purposes.

The Panchayati Raj accounting framework also distinguishes capital expenditure from revenue expenditure in budget as well as in the accounts. Capital expenditure is incurred with the object either of increasing concrete assets of permanent character or reducing recurring liabilities, and is generally met from receipts debt, deposit, etc. as distinguished from revenues derived from taxes, duties, fees, fines and similar items of current income including extraordinary receipts. However, it is open to the Panchayats to meet capital expenditure from revenue receipts provided there are sufficient revenue resources to cover it.

Revenue expenditure embraces all expenditure on working and upkeep of the project and also on renewals and replacements and additions, improvements or extensions as prescribed by Government.

3.3 NEED FOR CLASSIFICATION OF TRANSACTIONS

It is necessary that transactions should be classified under various heads and the results of transactions under these heads arranged in such a form as to show clearly not merely the significance of each transaction but also the combined effect of any desired series of transactions. This is achieved by opening a separate account for each head in the ledger about which we will learn in detail later.

The classification of transactions in Panchayat accounts has close reference to the programmes and activities of the Institutions and the object of the revenue and expenditure.

3.3.1 Unit of classification

The main unit of classification is the Major Head. Major Heads should be seen as the broad objective of the PRIs. Major Head classification with codes for the functions listed in Schedule XI is given in **ANNEXURE-II**. The functions are further classified under programmes, schemes and inputs. In the classification structure, the Major Head represents functions (distinct type of services) like General Education, Family Welfare, Roads, etc. The Sub-Major Head under the Major Head represents sub-heads like Elementary Education, Secondary Education under General Education. The Minor Head below Sub-Major Head represents a programme like Primary Schools, Secondary Schools under Elementary Education and Secondary Education respectively. The Sub-Head below Minor Head represents a scheme, the Detailed Head a sub-scheme and the Object Head, which is the last level of classification, constitutes inputs like salaries, wages, travel expenses, office expenses. The six-tier structure is exhibited in the Table below.

TABLE

Functions	Code of Classification	Example
Function	Major Head	Education
Sub-Function	Sub-Major Head	Elementary Education
Programme	Minor Head	Primary Schools
Scheme	Sub-Head	Sarva Shishka Abhiyan
Sub-Scheme/Activity	Detailed Head	Physical Activities
Object of Expenditure	Object Head	Salary, Office Expenses

Not all Institutions use all the levels of classification depending upon their need and budgeting system. However, it may be desirable to use detailed classification, as restricting the levels of classification could result in loss of detailed accounting information. The list of account heads upto Minor Head level for use by PRIs has been issued by the Comptroller & Auditor General of India in October 2002. State Governments have been entrusted with the function relating to the opening of heads of accounts to accommodate the schemes and sub-schemes below a programme head on the advice of the State Accountant General (A&E).

3.3.2 Codification of Heads of Accounts

Heads of account upto the Minor Head level have been assigned codes in numerals. Classification codes help identify types of transactions.

A four-digit code has been allotted to the Major Head (function).

- Codes beginning with 0 or 1 refer to Revenue Receipts
- Codes beginning with 2 or 3 refer to Revenue Expenditure

- Codes beginning with 4 or 5 refer to Capital Expenditure
- Codes beginning with 6 or 7 refer to Loans and Advances.

The other three digits represent the function and are the same in all sections. This is illustrated below-

Function		Receipt Head Revenue Account	Expenditure Head Revenue Account	Expenditure Head Capital Account	Loans and Advances
1.	General Education	0202	2202	4202	6202
2.	Medical & Public Health	0210	2210	4210	6210

A two-digit code 01, 02, etc. is allotted to a sub-Major Head (sub-function) and a Minor Head (programme) given a three-digit code 001, 002, etc. For minor heads having a common nomenclature under various Major/ sub-Major Heads, as far as possible. The same three digit code is adopted, e.g. 001 — Direction and Administration, 003 — Training, 004 Research, 050 Land. 0.52 — Machinery and Equipment. Each of the levels there-below, i.e. sub-Head below Minor Head, a Detailed Head below sub-Head and an Object Head below detailed head has a two digit code.

The two-digit code given to the scheme shall be unique irrespective of the fact that it appears under more than one Major Head (function). For the purpose of coding of schemes, all the schemes shall be cataloged in the first instance at the state level by the concerned administrative department. The identical schemes shall be grouped together to ensure that the code is unique to a particular scheme, even if it features under more than one function.

In order to identify a scheme to a particular source of funding, the two digit scheme code will be preceded by an additional one digit alpha code which could be 'A' for Government of India grants, 'B' for State Government grants, 'C' for Tenth Finance Commission funds, 'D' for Eleventh Finance Commission funds. 'E' for State Finance Commission funds. 'F' for State Plan funds, 'G' for Member Parliament Local Area Development Schemes and 'H' for MLA Local Area Development Schemes. Swarnjayanti Gram Swarojgar Yojana has been allotted 01 as a unique scheme code and is funded by Government of India. The classification code would be A01 and in case, it is funded by the State Government, the classification code would be B01, 'A' or 'B' representing source of financing i.e. Government of India or the State Government and 01 representing the unique scheme code.

The object head (inputs), for the sake of uniformity across the States have been standardised. The list of object heads with the standard code for each head is given as **Annexure-III** to be used across the State. These are used as primary units of appropriation. Itemised details of object head of expenditure like dearness allowance, house rent allowance, etc. under salaries may be kept outside accounts in the institutional records as per requirement.

3.3.3 Classification of Specific Items

Pay and Allowances

The pay and allowances of Panchayat employees are classified in accounts as part of scheme, activity or organisation (sub-head) under a programme (Minor Head) below a function (Major Head) to which services of the employees are closely related. Where, however, the duties of an employee extend to several activities, programmes, functions, etc. and it is not possible to classify *ab-initio* his/her pay and allowances under the appropriate sub-heads, the charges are classified part of the scheme or activity or organisation to which the major portion the work of the employee relates.

Travel Expenses

The travel expenses of an employee on whatever duty he/she may be employed are debited under the same major/minor/ sub-head as his/her pay. However, in cases where an employee is required to travel on duty connected with an outside body or fund or when it is considered necessary to show separately the cost a special service in connection with which the tour is undertaken, the travel expenses may be debited to a Major/Minor head, different from that to which his/her pay is debited.

Advance of traveling allowance is debited to the final head of account and shall be adjusted as revenue expenditure in the accounts of the Panchayat which makes the advance.

SUM - UP

1. Under Article 243J of the Constitution inserted vide Constitution (73rd Amendment) Act, 1992, the Legislature of the State may, by law, make provisions with respect to the maintenance of accounts by Panchayats. The head of account shall be opened in conformity with these rules and divergence. The receipt or expenditure shall be brought to account as determined by the

State Government in consultation with the State Accountant General (A&E).

2. The CAG, in order to have a uniform system of accounts maintenance across the country, based on the recommendations of the Eleventh Finance Commission (EFC) duly accepted by the Government of India, devised formats for the budget and the accounts for the Panchayati Raj Institutions (PRIs) in October 2002. There is a general consensus on the acceptability of these among the States.

3. The Panchayats accounting framework distinguishes between revenue and capital expenditure in the budget as well as accounts.

4. Transactions need to be classified under various heads and these heads need to be arranged in such a form as to show clearly not merely the significance of each transaction but also the combined effect of any desired series of transactions. In the classification structure, the Major Head represents functions (distinct type of services) like General Education, Family Welfare, Roads, etc. Sub-Major Head under the Major Head represents a sub-function like Elementary Education. Secondary Education under General Education. The Minor Head below Sub-Major Head represents a programme like Primary Schools, Secondary Schools under Elementary Education and Secondary Education respectively. The Sub-Head below Minor Head represents a scheme, the Detailed Head a sub-scheme and the Object Head, which is the last level of classification, constitutes inputs like salaries, wages, travel expenses, Office expenses.

5. Heads of account upto the Minor Head level have been assigned codes in Arabic numerals. Classification codes help identify types of transactions. For the purpose of coding of schemes, all the schemes shall be catalogued in the first instance at the state level by the concerned administrative department. The identical schemes shall be grouped together to ensure that the code is unique to a particular scheme, even if it features under more than one function.

6. The pay and allowances of Panchayat employees are classified in accounts as part of scheme, activity or organisation (sub-head) under a programme (Minor Head) below a function (Major Head) to which the services of the employee closely relate.

Chapter - 4

Accounting in Panchayati Raj Institutions

4.1 Major Principles

Let us have a recap of major principles governing accounting in PRIs.

- According to 73rd Constitutional Amendment Act, the state legislature may, by law, prescribe accounts and audit arrangements of Panchayati Raj Institutions. However, considering the state of maintenance of Panchayat accounts in different states, Eleventh Finance Commission recommended (2001) that the C&AG should prescribe the format for the preparation of budgets and for keeping accounts for the local bodies.
- Thirteenth Finance Commission (FC) recommended that while the CAG should provide technical guidance and supervision, a major portion of the actual auditing would have to be undertaken by the local fund audit departments. Hence, all State Governments should strengthen their local fund audit departments appropriately through both capacity building of existing manpower as well as augmentation of personnel. The Thirteenth FC also recommended adoption of NMAM for ULBs and Model Accounting System (MAS) for PRIs which was formulated /issued by the CAG in conjunction with the Union Ministry of Urban Development (now MoHUA) and Panchayati Raj respectively.
- In Fifteenth Finance Commission interim report (2020-21), the FC reiterated that timely availability of audited accounts separately

at the local body level and jointly at the State and all-India level continued to be a problem despite the emphasis laid by previous Commissions. The Fifteenth Finance Commission considered the availability of accounts online, both before and after audit, of all three levels of Government a critical reform agenda. The FC recommended that the upgraded PRIASoft software needs to be integrated with the Integrated Financial Management Information System (IFMIS/IFMS) of the State Governments (wherever it exists) and the Public Financial Management System (PFMS) of the CGA in the Union Government in order to generate online accounts by each rural local body, enable online auditing of such accounts and their consolidation at the State and all-India levels.

- Under Article 243J of the Constitution inserted vide Constitution (73rd Amendment) Act, 1992, the Legislature of the State may, by law, make provisions with respect to the maintenance of accounts by Panchayats. The head of account shall be opened in conformity with these rules and in case of divergence, the receipt or expenditure shall be brought to account as determined by the State Government in consultation with the State Accountant General (A&E).
- The CAG, to have a uniform system of accounts maintenance across the country, based on the recommendations of the Eleventh Finance Commission (EFC) duly accepted by the Government of India, devised formats for the budget and the accounts for the Panchayati Raj Institutions (PRIs) in October 2002. There is a general consensus on the acceptability of these formats among the States.
- Transactions need to be classified under various heads and these heads need to be arranged in such a form as to show clearly not merely the significance of each transaction but also the combined effect of any desired series of transactions. In the classification structure, the Major Head represents functions (distinct type of services) like General Education, Family Welfare, Roads, etc. The Sub-Major Head under the Major Head represents sub-function like Elementary Education, Secondary Education under General Education. The Minor Head below the Sub-Major Head represents a Programme like Primary Schools, Secondary Schools under Elementary Education and Secondary Education, respectively. The Sub-Head below Minor Head represents a

scheme, the Detailed Head a sub-scheme and the Object Head, which is the last level of classification, constitutes inputs like salaries, wages, travel expenses, office expenses.

- Heads of account upto the Minor Head level have been assigned codes in Arabic numerals. Classification codes help identify types of transactions. For the purpose of coding of schemes, all the schemes shall be catalogued in the first instance at the state level by the concerned administrative department. The identical schemes shall be grouped together to ensure that the code is unique to a particular scheme, even if it features under more than one function.
- The pay and allowances of Panchayat employees are classified in accounts as part of scheme, activity or organisation (sub-head) under a Programme (Minor Head) below a function (Major Head) to which the services of the employee closely relate.

4.2 Parts of PRI Accounts

The PRI accounts shall be kept in two parts:

- Part-I: Panchayat Funds; and
- Part-II: Debt (other than that included in Part-I), Deposits and Advances.

Part-I shall record receipts and expenditure on revenue account dealing with proceeds of taxation and other revenue receipts and expenditure met therefrom. It shall also record receipts on capital account which deals with receipts of capital nature which cannot be used for setting off the capital expenditure. Capital expenditure met with the object of either creating concrete· assets of material and permanent nature or reducing the recurring liabilities is recorded in Part-I. These apart, loans and advances made by Panchayats together with their recoveries and the loans raised by Panchayats and their repayment shall also be recorded in this part.

Part-II, transactions under debt, deposits and advances and remittances shall be recorded. Debt, deposits and advances are such in respect of which Panchayat involves a liability to repay the moneys received or has a claim to recover the amounts paid together with the repayment of former (debt and deposit) and the recoveries of the latter (advances). Remittances are merely adjusting heads and are booked temporarily until these are transferred to the correct/ final head of account.

Some of the transactions which may be booked in Part-II are: Panchayat Employees Provident Fund, Civil Deposits like security deposit by subordinates, earnest money made by intending tenderers, deposit by contractors, departmental advances, investment of cash balances, etc.

4.3 Accounting Records in PRIs

To appreciate the PRI functioning and how to keep the accounts, it is imperative that we learn about basic accounting records – nature of bills and vouchers, the subsidiary registers, the forms of cheques and forms and content of Cash Book. These records are necessarily to be maintained at various levels of PRIs.

4.3.1 Bills, Vouchers and Challans

A **bill** is a statement of claims against Panchayat containing specifications of the nature and amount of the claim either in total or by items and includes such a statement presented in the form of a receipt. A bill becomes a **voucher** when it is passed for payment, paid, receipted and stamped.

Officers entrusted with the payment of money shall obtain for every payment they make, including repayment of sums previously lodged with Panchayats, a voucher setting forth full particulars of the claim and all information necessary for its proper classification and identification in the accounts. Every voucher shall bear, or have attached to it, an acknowledgement for the payment signed by the person by whom, or on whose behalf, the claim is put forth. The acknowledgement shall be taken at the time of payment. In respect of adjustment bills, however, it is not necessary to insist upon an acknowledgement as it does not involve any payment.

Guidelines for Preparation of Bills

The following guidelines shall be kept in view while preparing bills:

Prescribed printed forms shall, as far as possible, be used.

(i) Bills shall be filled in ink and signed in ink. Making entries and signatures with ball pens is permissible unless prohibited under specific rules or orders.

(ii) The amount of each bill shall, as far as whole Rupees are concerned, be written in words as well as in figures. The fraction of a Rupee may, however, be written in figures after writing Rupees in words.

(iii) All corrections and alterations in the amount of the bill whether in words or figures shall be attested over full and dated signature.

(iv) Erasers and overwritings are forbidden and shall be avoided. In case it becomes necessary to make a correction, the incorrect entry shall be cancelled and the correct entry inserted in red ink.

(v) Complete accounts classification shall be recorded on each bill.

(vi) Charges against two or more major heads shall not be included in one bill.

(vii) Orders sanctioning charges included in the bill shall be quoted and a copy of the sanction attached to the bill.

(viii) All bills shall be entered in the Drawal Register.

(ix) Bills for telephone charges, water and electricity charges affixed with facsimile signature of the authorised officer, unsigned bills prepared on computers forming sub-vouchers for the bills for contingent charges may be accepted for payment, if otherwise in order.

(x) As a general rule preparation of a duplicate or a copy of a bill is prohibited unless duplicates have to be prepared by any rule or order. Payment on a duplicate or a copy of the bill shall not be made.

Bills drawn up and presented for payment by departmental officers shall themselves bear receipt for payment. Separate receipts, duly affixed with revenue stamp, wherever necessary, shall be obtained and furnished to the paying authority at the time of receiving payment in respect of all other payments claimed through bills.

Remittance Challans

PRIs, through State Legislation, are authorised to levy, collect and appropriate some taxes, duties, tolls and fees. They are also assigned some taxes, duties and tolls levied and collected by the State Government and given grants-in-aid by the State Government. Revenues, dues and other money receivable by Panchayats may be realised in cash, or by cheques or drafts, or in any form provided in the rules. Revenues and dues may be received directly or by the accredited bank branch in the form of local cheques or drafts or in cash.

Any party or person paying money into the bank on account of amounts payable to Panchayats shall present it with a document called **'challan'** in duplicate, triplicate or quadruplicate as specified in rules in the prescribed form.

Guidelines for Challan preparation

(i) Challans should show the nature of payment, the office on whose account it is made and complete account classification of the credit.

(ii) Separate challans shall be used for moneys creditable to different heads of account.

(iii) Where money is received, the payer shall be given a receipt duly signed. The receipt shall indicate the amount in words as well as in figures.

(iv) Receipts shall be machine numbered and the receipt book kept in the personal custody of the officer authorised to sign the receipt.

(v) A formal receipt for payment by cheque shall be given after the cheque has been cleared. In the event of cheque being dishonoured, the tenderer shall be informed with a demand to make the payment in cash and the dishonoured cheque returned.

4.3.2 Cash Book

The Cash Book is the primary and most important record for keeping accounts of moneys received and payments made. All Panchayats shall maintain cash book in the prescribed form. All transactions, whether in cash or by cheque shall be entered in chronological order in the cash book as soon as they occur and attested by officer-in-charge of cash book of the Panchayat. On the left-hand side of the cash book, all moneys received in cash, by cheques, bank drafts, etc. shall be entered while on the right-hand side all payments by cash or cheques shall be recorded. The accounting classification shall be written in each case. A cheque issued outside the headquarters is entered in the cash book on return to headquarters. The date on which it is entered in the cash book is shown as numerator and the actual date of issue as denominator.

In village Panchayat, Panchayat Secretary maintains cash book under the direction and guidance of the Gram Panchayat/Pradhan. In the Block Panchayat/ Panchayat Samiti and the District Panchayat/ Zilla Parishad cash book is maintained by an Accountant under the directions and guidance of the Drawing & Disbursing Officer (DDO) nominated for the purpose.

Maintenance of cash book

The following guidelines may be kept in view in respect of the maintenance of cash book by panchayats.

- The cash book shall be bound and pages machine numbered.
- Before bringing the cash book in use, the officer-in-charge or the Secretary and the Pradhan in the case of Village Panchayats should count the number of pages and record a certificate regarding number of pages contained therein on the first page of cash book.
- The cash book shall be written, closed and checked on day-to-day basis.
- The maximum cash in hand should not exceed the prescribed limit at any time. All the surplus cash should be deposited into the bank/treasury.
- At the close of the day, it should be seen that the receipts collected during the day are deposited into the bank on the same day or on the morning of the next day.
- The totaling in the cash book shall be verified by some responsible subordinate officer other than the writer of the cash book who shall initial it as correct.
- An eraser or overwriting of an entry in the cash book is prohibited. If a mistake is discovered, it shall be corrected by drawing a pen through the incorrect entry and inserting the correct in red ink between the lines. The correction shall be attested over the date signatures.
- Panchayats are authorised to draw cheques and make payments by cheques. Once the cheque is issued the expenditure is recorded in the cash book even though the cheque may not be encashed in the same accounting period.
- The closing bank/treasury balance as per cash book shall be compared with the balances as per bank passbook/statement/ treasury passbook and a monthly reconciliation statement drawn up on the last working day of the month.

- Cash, cheque drafts, etc. shall be kept in safe custody in cash chest or almirah.
- At the time of transfer of the cashier or the officer-in-charge of cash book proper handing over of cash balances shall be made under the dated signature. Note of this effect shall be kept in the cash book.
- Use of Panchayat receipts for Panchayat expenditure is prohibited. If it is considered expedient to make use of receipts for current expenditure, before the end of the month cheque should be drawn by transfer credit to Panchayat.

Verification of Cash Balance

At the end of the month, the officer-in-charge or Secretary in the case of Village Panchayat, as the case may be, shall

(a) Verify the cash balance in the chest with the cash balance in 'cash' column on receipt side of the cash book and give a certificate.

(b) Also compare every item of receipt and expenditure as shown in the bank passbook/ statement of Treasury passbook with the relevant entries of the corresponding month in the cash book. The difference, if any, shall be explained and accounted for in footnote in the cash book.

(c) A surprise check of cash shall also be conducted by the Executive Officer or Secretary once or twice a month to ensure that cash in hand agrees with the cash book. As and when a check is made, a certificate of count shall be recorded in the cash book.

(d) If on comparison of the cash book with the Treasury passbook any cheque appears to be unduly long outstanding, enquiries shall be made regarding it and if it cannot be traced its payment shall be stopped by the order of the Drawing Officer.

4.3.3 Cheques and the related Records

4.3.3.1 Cheque and its Essential Features

Section 6 of the Negotiable Instruments Act, as amended by the Negotiable Instruments (Amendment) Act, 2002 (effective from 6th Feb. 2003) defines a cheque as a bill of exchange drawn on a specified banker and not expressed to be payable otherwise than on demand. Further, the expression includes the electronic usage of a cheque in the electronic form.

Cheques are used for withdrawing money from the bank or for making payments through the bank. The officer who is authorised to draw cheques shall send his/ her specimen signatures to the treasury/ bank upon which he draws money. The Administrator in the case of personal deposit account/ drawing officer shall notify to the Treasury/ Bank upon which he/ she draws, the number of each cheque book from time to time, which he brings into use and the number of cheques it contains. All cheques issued shall be entered in the Cheques Issue Register.

The person who draws the cheque (the account holder or the authorised person) is called 'drawer', the bank on whom the cheque is drawn is called 'drawee', and the person in whose favour the cheque is drawn is known as the 'payee'.

The essential features of a cheque are as under:

1. **Written instrument:** A cheque is an instrument in writing. In India, bankers did not encourage writing of cheques with ball pens.

2. **Unconditional order:** A cheque must contain an unconditional order.

3. **On a specified banker only:** A cheque is drawn on a specified banker whose name and address is usually printed on the cheque.

4. **A certain sum of money:** The order must be only for the payment of a sum of money duly specified in the cheque.

5. **Payee to be certain:** A cheque can be a bearer cheque or an order cheque. In case of **a bearer cheque,** bank pays the amount to any person who presents it at the counter of the payee bank without much fuss. Of course, the bank gets his/her name and signatures at the back of the cheque and in case the amount involved is large, it insists on identification. In case of an order cheque, it is payable to a specified person or his order. The term 'person' includes individuals, partnership firms, a company, a body corporate, local authority, clubs, institutions, etc. The words 'or order' implies that the person specified in the cheque can transfer the cheque to any person by endorsing it in his name. Of course, this is not possible in case of Account Payee Cheques.

6. **Payable on demand:** Cheque must be payable on demand and not otherwise. Use of the words "on demand" or their equivalent is not necessary. When the drawer asks the banker to pay and does not specify the time for its payment, the instrument is

payable on demand (Section 19 of Negotiable Instruments Act). However, the cheque has a validity period (three to six months) within which it must be presented, otherwise it becomes stale (out of date) and its payment is refused.

7. **Amount of cheques:** Amount of the cheque must be clearly mentioned. The amount should be written both in words as well as in figures to avoid any doubt. Moreover, the amount should be so written as to leave no blank space before or after the words and end with the word 'only'.
8. **Dating of cheques:** The drawer of a cheque is expected to date it before it leaves his hands. A cheque without a date is considered incomplete and is returned unpaid by the bank. The drawer can date a cheque even with a date later than the date on which it is drawn. Such a cheque is called **Post-Date Cheque.** A post-date cheque cannot be honoured except at the personal risk of the bank's manager, till the date mentioned. A post-date cheque is as much negotiable as a cheque for which payment is due i.e. the transferee of a post-date cheque, like that of the cheque on which payment is due, acquires a better title than its transferor, if he is holder in due course.
9. **Period of validity of a cheque:** Cheques shall be payable at any time within three/six months after the month of issue/ date of issue (as per the local instruction).

If the currency of a cheque expires owing to its not being presented at the bank within its validity period, it may be received back by the drawer who shall cancel it over his signature and issue a fresh cheque in lieu thereof. Entries about cancellation of old cheque and issue of a fresh cheque shall be made in the counterfoil of the old cheque, in the Cheques Issue Register, in the bills, and the list of outstanding cheques.

A few important rules relating to issue of cheques to be followed by Panchayati Raj officials are as follows:

1. No cheque shall be signed for issue unless required for immediate delivery.
2. The validity of the cheque indicating the number of months from the date of issue or month of issue shall be recorded on the top of the same.
3. Self Cheque is permitted to replenish cash for chest.

4. The minimum amount for which the cheque may be issued must be prescribed with exception, if any.
5. Cheque towards payment of personal claims and claims of contractors and suppliers must be drawn as payable to or order of the payee.

Registers related to Cheque Books

Cheque books received from the accredited bank shall be recorded in a **Register of Cheque Books**. Issuance of a cheque book shall be noted in the Register under proper attestation and book number notified to the bank/ treasury before the same is brought into use. The Register of cheque books is maintained to keep a watch on the receipt and issue of cheque books.

Cheques issued shall be entered in a **Cheques Issue Register** under proper attestation.

4.3.4 Register of Contingent Expenditure

Contingent expenditure refers to all incidental and other expenses, including those on stores, which are incurred for the management of an office other than those specifically classified as falling under some other head of expenditure. A Register of Contingent Expenditure shall be kept by each Panchayat to enable the disbursing officer to watch the progress of the expenditure under each object head as compared with the appropriation for it. Entries made in the Register shall be initialed by the authorised functionary drawing the contingent bill.

The contingent bill shall be accompanied by sub-vouchers, payees receipt(s), supplier bill(s) containing details of supplies made or the services rendered for which payments are required to be made. As each payment is made, entries shall be recorded in the Register. All paid vouchers and supply bills are defaced, cancelled and stamped as paid to avoid double claim/ payment.

The recipient of the material shall record a certificate in the bill to the effect that material have been received in good condition and have been entered at appropriate page in the stock register.

A progressive total of all the object heads shall be worked out monthly. As appropriation of funds is indicated in the Register, it shows the availability of funds and serves as a tool for an effective control over expenditure.

4.3.5 Demand and Collection Register

The Demand and Collection Register is maintained to ensure that the various levies, taxes, fees and other amounts due to Panchayats are demanded and collected on time. Panchayats shall be responsible to ensure that all sums due to them are regularly and promptly assessed, realised and credited to the account of the Panchayat. Detailed rules and procedure regarding assessment, collection, allocation, remission and abandonment of revenue could be found in the local Panchayat manuals.

When the PRIs receive moneys, a receipt shall be issued over the signature of an authorised person, and the authorised functionary shall maintain a separate register for each category of demand.

A Register of Assesses as identified by the Panchayats and approved by Gram Sabha/ Officer-in-charge of other Panchayats shall also be maintained.

The Register shall also be maintained in cases where the work of collection of Panchayat's dues is done by the outside agencies appointed for the purpose. All moneys received shall be brought to account forthwith in the cash book and credited into accredited bank by the authorised functionaries or agency receiving such money.

4.3.6 Register of Lands

All lands transferred by government, purchased, acquired by or vested with Panchayats shall be entered in the Register of Lands indicating the date of transfer, purchase, acquisition, purpose, cost of land with survey number, etc. Details of structures, if any, acquired with the land and the utilisation of the structure and the land shall also be noted in the Register. For any form of transfer of land, the authority for the same shall be recorded in the Register under proper attestation.

4.3.7 Register of Roads

All roads vesting with the Panchayats and those constructed from time to time shall be entered in the Register of Roads indicating the details of location and other particulars for their clear identification.

4.3.8 Register of Immovable Properties other than Lands and Roads

All immovable properties, comprising plantation, tanks and ponds, buildings, etc. vesting in the Panchayats shall be entered in the Register of Immovable Properties. These properties shall be physically verified annually by an independent authorised officer. The verifying officer/ person shall record a certificate indicating the results of his verification. A certificate as to whether the properties are being utilised for the intended purposes and are being maintained properly shall also be recorded. In case the immovable item is not being utilised, the fact shall be reported to the competent authority.

This is a permanent register and shall be kept in the personal custody of a responsible authority of the respective Panchayat.

4.3.9 Register of Movable Properties/ Stores

All movable properties and stores of the permanent or durable nature such as furniture, books, equipment and machinery, vehicles, carts, etc. belonging to Panchayat shall be recorded article-wise in the Register of Movable Properties under the initials of the competent/ authorised functionary. When the property is disposed off finally, by sale or otherwise, the particulars of disposal shall be also recorded in the Register under the initials of the competent functionary.

The Register is intended to be a permanent record and shall be kept under the personal supervision of competent authority. Articles of movable property/ stores shall be verified physically at least once in a year and the result recorded on the register by an officer other than the custodian of the stock/ store.

4.3.10 Register of Loans Received

For the loans received, a Register of Loans Received shall be maintained. For the loans disbursed, another register called Register of Loans Disbursed shall be maintained, separate pages being allotted to different classes or categories of loans. Recovery of the loans shall be monitored through this Register and demand for recovery compiled periodically. Loan-wise files shall also be maintained. These would contain:

(i) Name and address of loanee

(ii) Details of sanction/ authority for loan

(iii) Purpose of loan

(iv) Conditions attached

(v) Terms of repayment and rate of interest

(vi) Details of security obtained along with the connected documents

To ensure that loans disbursed, and the recoveries effected are properly classified and accounted for, a broadsheet known as Broadsheet of Loans Received/Disbursed shall be maintained. The broadsheet shall be completed after the month's accounts have been compiled. The entries in the broadsheet shall be made from the Register of Loans Disbursed, and the corresponding figures of loans disbursed taken from accounts. In case of any difference, the same shall be reconciled and, before the accounts for the year are finally closed, all differences are finally cleared.

4.3.11 Register of Inventory of Works/Assets

Each Panchayat should maintain a Register of Inventory of Works/ Assets created under various schemes detailing therein the date of approval by Gram Sabha, Block and District Panchayats, date of commencement and completion, expenditure incurred, name and area, reference to the entry in Register of Immovable Property, date of completion certificates, etc. The work/ assets should be physically verified by an independent authorised functionary/ officer to see whether the completed works/ assets are in existence and are being maintained properly.

Necessary action shall be taken against functionary in all cases where the works/ assets are found to be of sub-standard quality and or non-existent. The register shall be a consolidated one on a continuous basis to have the details of up-to-date assets created by respective Panchayats from time to time.

4.3.12 Register of Receipts

All revenue receipts and other realisations including Government grants and those appearing in the bank's daily scroll or treasury passbook shall be entered in the Register of Receipts. Enough pages shall be allotted to each major head of receipt in the Register.

Daily and progressive figures of receipts under each head shall be worked out. At the end of the month, the effect of correction through transfer entry carried out during the month shall be posted in the Register to arrive at monthly total under each head. Progressive total shall be carried forward from month to month so that total annual receipts under each head are available.

4.3.12 Register of Expenditure

A Register of Expenditure shall be maintained for recording the payments made every day. Enough pages shall be allotted to each major head of expenditure in the Register. Daily and progressive figures of expenditure under each head shall be worked out. At the end of the month, the effect of correction through transfer entry carried out during the month shall be posted in the Register to arrive at monthly total under each head. Progressive total shall be carried forward from month to month so that total annual expenditure under each head are available.

Form of accounts for various books and registers are given in **Annexure IV**.

4.4 Formats Prescribed by CAG of India

We have discussed in detail the records to be maintained by PRIs. These records are required to maintain transparency in financial transactions in PRIs. In addition to the above, following statements are required to be prepared annually in the proforma modeled by the Comptroller & Auditor General of India. Formats are given in **Annexure V**. We are going to discuss these formats as below:

4.4.1 Monthly Receipts and Payments Account

Monthly Receipts and Payments Account shows the total amounts received and paid during and upto the end of the month duly classified major head-wise as also the budget estimates for the year. This account has two sides to record receipts and payments under various functional heads of account on left and right-hand side respectively. To start with, on the receipt side, opening balance (cash in hand, balance in bank/ treasury, investments and their total) is recorded. The Receipts side has four columns, namely (i) head of account, (ii) budget estimates for the current year, (iii) actuals during the month, and (iv) receipts upto the end of the month. Similarly, the payment side is also divided into four columns; namely, heads of account, budget estimates for the year, actuals during the month and expenditure at the end of the month. At the end, the closing balance of cash in hand, balance in bank/ treasury, investments and total thereof is worked out and shown on the payment side. The grand totals of the receipt side and the payment side must be equal. This implies correctness of the accounts.

It may be noted that its closing balance is compared with the balance as per cash book and the one reported in the bank passbook. In case of any difference, the same is analysed in the monthly Reconciliation Statement.

4.4.2 Annual Receipts and Payments Account

Annual Receipt and Payment Account is just like the Monthly

Receipts and Payments Account, and shows the amount received and paid during the year (period of account), classified functionally upto the object head, as also the opening and the closing balances. It also shows the corresponding amounts for the previous year and incorporates the budget estimates under various functions upto the primary level of appropriation to facilitate the comparison of amounts spent vis-à-vis budget provision and take note of the variances.

4.4.3 Statements forming part of Accounts

Besides drawing up annual Receipt and Payment Account, the following statements shall be prepared and appended to the account:

4.4.3.1 Statement of Capital Expenditure

The statement will record capital expenditure during the year and upto the end of the year for all schemes (function-wise) executed by the Panchayat.

4.4.3.2 Statement of Receivables and Payables

The statement is intended to give head-wise (aggregate for each spending unit) details of all receivables and payables for the year.

4.4.3.3 Statement of Balances under Deposits, Advances and Loans

Receipts and payments pertaining to deposits, advances and loans for the whole year would be recorded in the statement under the following headings:

- Head of account

Under this column, major and minor items of deposits, advances and loans are shown vertically and, at the end, total under each major head of account worked-out

- opening balance (closing balances from the similar statement for the previous year)
- Receipts during the year
- Payments during the year
- Closing balance at the end of the year
- Detailed description of investments

Adverse or minus closing balances under any head of account shall be explained in the footnote.

4.4.3.4 Statement of Provident Funds and Investments

Receipts, payments, interest earned and their investments for the year are shown under each head of account.

4.4.3.5 Monthly Reconciliation Statement

It is essential to tally the two sets of balances viz., the bank balance shown by the cash book and the balance shown by the bank passbook/ statement. In case of difference, it is equally essential to identify the reasons for the difference. To ensure that the bank balance shown by the cash book agrees with the balance shown in the bank passbook/statement, monthly preparation of the bank reconciliation statement is essential. The reconciliation brings out errors, which might have been crept in the cash book or the bank passbook/ statement. Regular and systematic reconciliation discourages the staff from committing irregularities including fraud/embezzlements, which due to lack of reconciliation remain undetected. A copy of the bank reconciliation statement shall be attached to monthly accounts.

4.5 Destruction of Records

No records connected with accounts shall be destroyed except in accordance with the general or special rules or orders applicable to Panchayats as prescribed in the Panchayat manuals. Preservation of accounts records in public works units shall be as prescribed by State Governments. The details of records destroyed under the orders of the competent authority shall be kept in each Panchayat. Before any pay bill/ pay bill register is destroyed, the services of the employees shall be duly verified.

It may be noted that the following records shall not be destroyed:

(i) Records connected with expenditure which is within the period of limitation fixed by law.

(ii) Records connected with expenditure on schemes or works not completed although beyond the period of limitation.

(iii) Records in respect of which audit objection is outstanding.

(iv) Records connected with claims to service and personal matters affecting persons in services.

(v) Orders and sanctions of a permanent character.

4.6 Digitalization of Accounting and Maintenance of Manual Records

The Ministry of Panchayati Raj has designed e-GramSwaraj application as a one stop portal for capturing all activities and accounting and financial information for all levels of PRIs.

We are going to learn about the features and uses of this portal in the next two chapters. The portal is quite comprehensive and in days to come may even replace the physical accounting and managerial information. However, as of now, the maintenance of physical records as discussed in this chapter are necessary for control and transparency purposes. Understanding the formats and principles behind these records are essential for appreciating PRI accounting. These records form the basis of digitalization also.

Chapter - 5

Introduction to Egramswaraj – Portal as Management Information System

EGRAMSWARAJ -A PORTAL

e-GramSwaraj is a digital platform that enables rural communities to access information and government services through a single portal. This initiative is aimed at promoting self-governance and rural development by empowering citizens to participate in decision-making processes. The e-GramSwaraj Yojana was launched in April 2020 by the Ministry of Panchayati Raj.

The goal of the e-GramSwaraj site is to increase transparency in job accounting, decentralised planning, and progress reporting. The e-GramSwaraj site is a single interface that maintains track of panchayats and offers work records from planning to implementation. It contains work details for each village panchayat identified in the Gram Panchayat Development Plan (GPDP). Anyone may access information about the panchayat's funding, development projects, and operations through this portal.

e-GramSwaraj is designed keeping the following **3 key target user groups** in consideration:

1. **Local Bodies**: Rural and Urban local bodies, together, forms up the primary end users of this application. These users, working at the field level, are primary custodians of numerous critical processes such as formulation of Gram Panchayat Development Plan (GPDP), Works progress monitoring, Vendor and employee management, and Financial Management.

2. **Line Departments:** GPDP cuts across 29 subjects and 18 Ministries of Government of India. These Line Departments are responsible for driving various social welfare programmes and schemes. Data driven Planning and Monitoring, naturally, forms the foundation of successful, last-mile, service delivery, especially for robust financial management.

3. **Citizens**: While the Gram Panchayat is operated by the elected and selected representatives of the citizens and administration respectively, it is the right and more importantly, the responsibility, of each and every citizen to be vigilant and aware of the status of progress and development taking place in their region. Equipped with ratified and readily available data, the general population plays a significant role in inclusive decision-making process.

FEATURES OF EGRAMSWARAJ INITIATIVE

The e-GramSwaraj initiative has several features that make it an effective tool for rural development. Some of these features are:

1. **Single Window Access:** The e-GramSwaraj portal provides citizens with access to multiple government services and information through a single window.

2. **Real-Time Monitoring:** The platform enables real-time monitoring of various activities and programmes implemented by the government at the local level.

3. **Mobile App:** The e-GramSwaraj mobile app provides citizens with access to government services and information on the go.

4. **Online Training:** The initiative also provides online training to rural communities on various topics related to self-governance and rural development.

5. **User-Friendly Interface:** The platform has a user-friendly interface that makes it easy for citizens to access government services and information.

Even though, the visible objective of this application is providing information to various users including the government, the stakeholders and the citizens in general, the core is Work Based Accounting Application.

So e-GramSwaraj application has two major interfaces:

1. Management Information System

2. Work-based accounting application

In this chapter, we will discuss the utility of this application as Management Information System for external stakeholders including the general public. The basic tenets of this comprehensive application can be understood in six categories:

(a) Panchayat Profiling
(b) Finance and Accounting
(c) Action Plan Creation
(d) Activity Output
(e) Geo-Tagging of Assets
(f) Progress Reporting

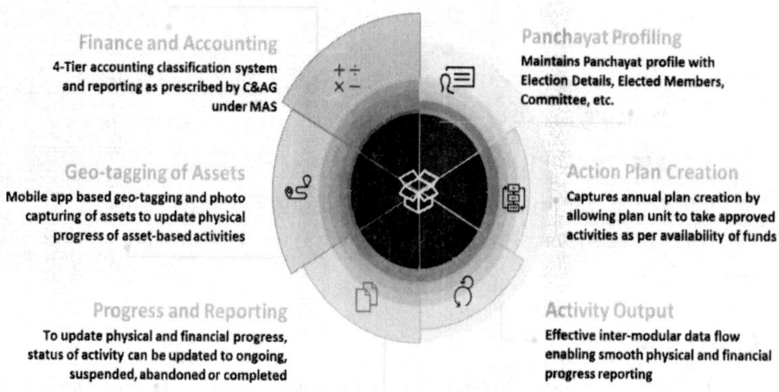

A. Panchayat Profile

This dashboard provides detailed information about all panchayats at various levels – like Gram Panchayat, Taluka Panchayat and District Panchayat.

This profile includes information on the selected panchayat, elected representatives' details, committee details etc. The LGD Code, which is the identifier is part of the profile. It is expected that in near future, this profile will also have status of service delivery in the selected Panchayat.

B. Planning Report

This dashboard gives a complete view of all planned and implemented activities. This module has been designed in four parts

- **Planning**

This module supports preparation of action plan, its approval, activity details sector-wise and theme-wise. Some of the important reports under this category are:

- ► Approved Action Plan Report
- ► Pending Action Plan Report
- ► List of Activities
- ► Activity Details Report

- **Reporting**

This module provides a summary of all activities undertaken by panchayats. Panchayat-wise expenditure report, scheme-wise activity status report and beneficiary report are some of the crucial reports.

- **Asset**

The third module relates to creation of data base of assets panchayat-wise.

- **Orientation Details**

The final module under the Planning Report dashboard is about creating awareness about e-GramSwaraj in States and orientation of stakeholders.

C. Accounting

For our purpose, this is the most important and most comprehensive module. This module has been titled Financial Progress Report and has been structured in six parts.

- All India Report
- MAS Registers
- Accounting Entity Wise Report
- Miscellaneous Report
- PFMS Integration Report
- GEM Integration Report

We are going to focus on only two categories, which are: (a) Accounting Entity Wise – in a detailed manner (b) MAS registers in a limited manner.

ACCOUNTING ENTITY WISE REPORT

This module is the core of e-GramSwaraj application. It is the digital version of accounting records and reports. All the basic records and flow of financial transactions have been captured in a detailed fashion.

The basic document or the first building block of any financial transaction is a voucher. It is a basic record for any transaction, whether it is revenue or expenditure. This category of Financial Report Module deals with all reports/ account books required for preparing accounts of the Panchayat. These are:

1. Day Book

As the name suggests, the Day Book is a descriptive and chronological record of each Day's transactions. It can also be called a book of original entry.

Receipts

It would contain details of all receipts in favour of Panchayat that day against the appropriate head of account. Receipts would be in the form of Remittance Challan, if paid by the individuals. Alternately, receipts would be in the form of Sanction order, if received from State or Central Government authorities.

Expenditure

It would also have details of all bills paid by the Panchayats. A Bill is a statement of claims against Panchayat containing specifications of the nature and amount of claim. A Bill becomes a voucher when it is passed for payment, paid, receipted and stamped.

To sum up, the Day Book is the summary of financial transactions of a Day.

2. Cash Book Report

Cash Book is the most important primary record for keeping account of money received and payments made by panchayats. Panchayat accounts are maintained on single entry and cash basis.

The structure of Cash Book, the formats and the rules of preparing these are covered in the earlier unit.

Under the e-GramSwaraj portal, Cash Book is derived from the Day Book and follows the formats prescribed in the physical accounting system. However, the option of having multiple Cash Book is possible. These are:

- Month-Wise or Scheme-Wise
- Accounting Entity-wise district, Intermediate or village panchayat

3. Account-wise Cash Book Report

This report is a detailed version of Cash Book and provides disaggregated information. It is an effective tool for decision-making and management information system. The components of this report are:

- Financial Year
- State and District
- Accounting Entity – District Panchayat/Intermediate Panchayat/ Village Panchayat
- Period of Report – Month-wise/ Date Range-wise
- Details of Account- Bank/Treasury/Post Office
- Scheme- Name of the Scheme
- Component of the Scheme

This report provides a bird's eye view of all receipts and payments as per the selected parameters.

4. O&M Expenditure Report

The operations and maintenance expenditure report is meant to keep the O&M component within the prescribed limits. The report provides information in following categories:

- Consolidated O & M heads
- O &M Head-wise
- Consolidated Expenditure Heads

5. Bank/Scheme-wise List of Accounts

This Report gives a summarised list of Bank or Scheme-wise accounts. It is a control statement

6. Receipt Analysis Report

Receipt Analysis Report gets created from the Cash Book entries and provides information

- Accounting Entity-wise
- For Selected Periods
- For Selected Source of Revenue
- For Range of Values
- Object Head-wise

7. Expenditure Analysis Report

This Report gives similar information as at six above, but for the expenditure items.

8. Ledger Book Report

Ledger Book is a collection of accounts; it can be depicted as the book of final entry. It would start with an opening balance; all additions and deductions would be recorded, and a closing balance would be arrived at.

9. Journal Book Report

In contrast, the Journal Book would be a running record of all financial transactions. The balance from the Journal Book would be transferred to Ledger Book.

MASTER ACCOUNTING SYSTEM REGISTERS

Master Accounting System is the next important module of Financial Progress Report. We have discussed the Accounting Entity-wise Reports above which are original input and output formats. The MAS Registers are the next step. These Registers provide a complete picture of both flow and stock transactions. These registers are crucial for control and backbone of financial records. These are:

1. Annual Receipts and Payments Accounts
2. Consolidated Abstract Register
3. Monthly Reconciliation Statement
4. Inventory (stock) Register
5. Register of Demand Collection and Balance

These registers are in line with the formats recommended by CAG, which we have discussed in earlier chapters. These registers are created from the inputs added in Accounting Entity-wise registers.

These Registers provide a consolidated view of all financial transactions and can be used to monitor activities of PRIs at various levels.

Let us look at features of one of these registers in e-GramSwaraj application.

- **Annual Receipts and Payments Accounts**

The format gives option of reporting at two levels:

- Financial Year Wise
- Month Wise

So this format serves the dual purpose of informing Monthly Receipt & Payments Account and Annual Receipt & Payment Account. The consolidation of financial transactions at minor head, sub-head or object head levels.

Other registers are maintained in similar formats as we discussed in manual formats.

The power of this application lies in providing information in a holistic fashion across States, at various levels of PRIs and aggregated and segregated views.

SUM-UP

The Dashboard of e-GramSwaraj would provide 360 degree view of PRI functioning – financial as well as functional when all data is inputted by all stakeholders.

Chapter - 6

E-Gramswaraj Portal as Work Based Accounting Application

We have discussed the use of e-GramSwaraj portal as the management information system in the earlier chapter. We have seen that this portal has the capability of providing comprehensive information for all stakeholders including the general public, elected representatives or administrators. It is also a platform for accessing information across Panchayats, Districts and States. To that extent, it is a treasure of information helping the core objective of PRIs.

At a more practical level, this portal serves as the core accounting application for the PRIs. This application provides various input formats and reporting formats for arriving at various reports which we have seen in the previous chapter.

In this chapter we are going to discuss the core accounting application-how to record and report financial transactions in PRIs. This application has the capability of capturing transactions across receipt and expenditure types – whether Central, State, or Own, however presently it is being used in most of the States for Central Government funds and schemes.

As this part is about working on an application, the study material is being presented as a Power Point presentation. The application is very user friendly and can only be accessed by authorised users after login through a user ID. It has features relating to adding records and transactions, editing and preparing reports.

E GRAMSWARAJ- Accounting application for PRIs

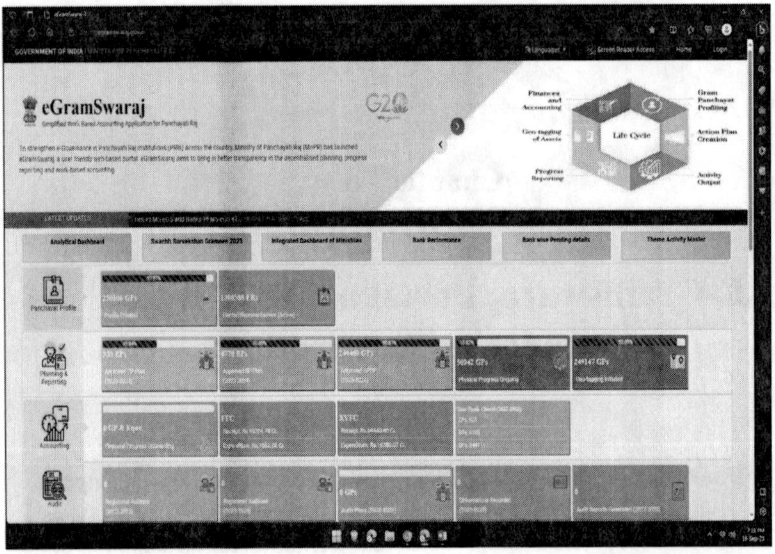

This is the introductory page, there are many links available related to the reporting section which can be used by Public to see panchayat profiles, schemes' expenditure, receipts and progress.

For accounting purposes, and to enter any data relating to expenditure and receipt, various functionaries have been given IDs and Passwords by the Ministry of Panchayati Raj.

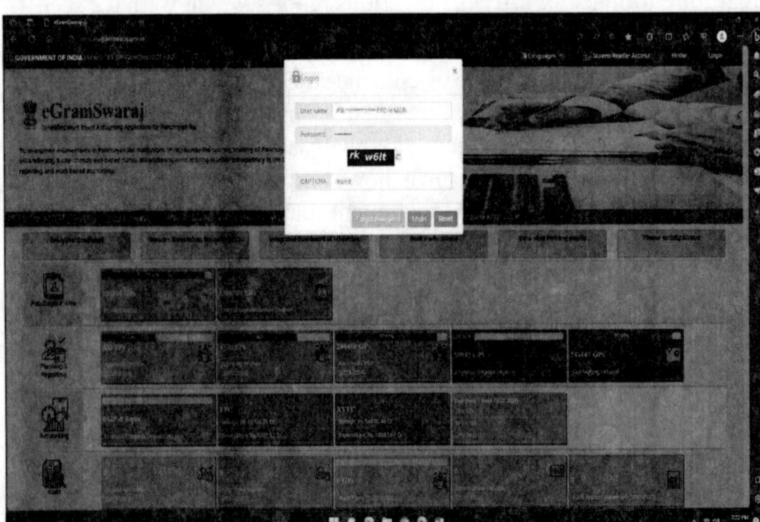

After log in, next Screen brings us to the Main Menu. There are eight subsections on the Main Menu

- Voucher Transactions
- Receipt Voucher
- Payment Voucher
- Create Voucher
- Journal Voucher
- Period End Procedures
- Master Entry
- Report

We will discuss all the above in upcoming slides.

Voucher Transactions has following sub-menus

1. Receipt Voucher
2. Payment Voucher
3. Contra Voucher
4. Journal Voucher

1. Receipt Voucher

It gives option of adding or managing a receipt voucher. All details like type, amount, received from, date and other particulars are filled here. This is one of the basic documents for accounting.

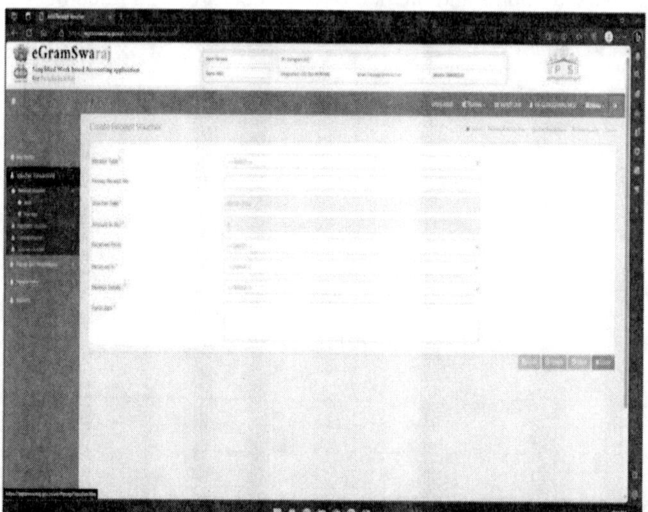

A form will appear when you click on Add in Receipt Voucher you have to properly fill the form to enter any Income entry.

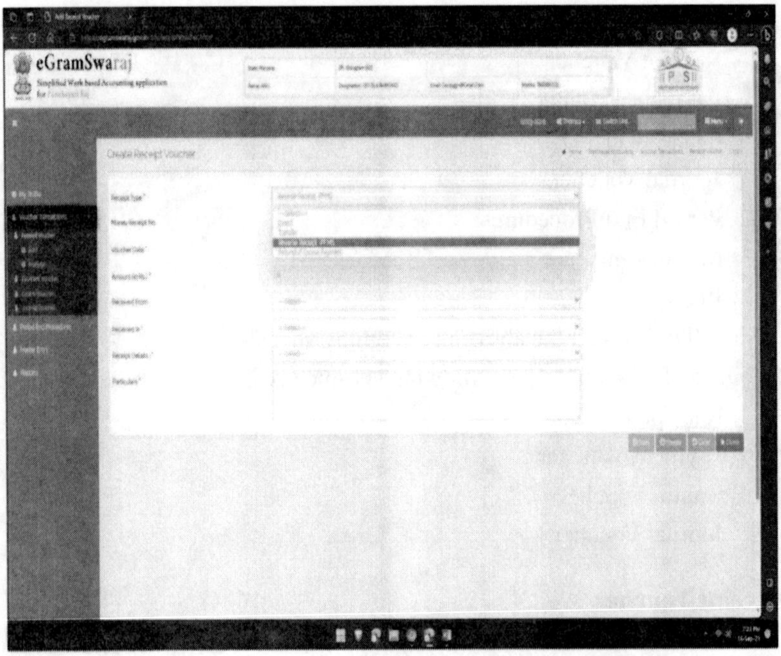

Similar as in receipt vouchers while entering expenditure a payment voucher has to be made. All details like the nature of payment, the related work, invoice numbers, amounts and method of payments are to be filled in.

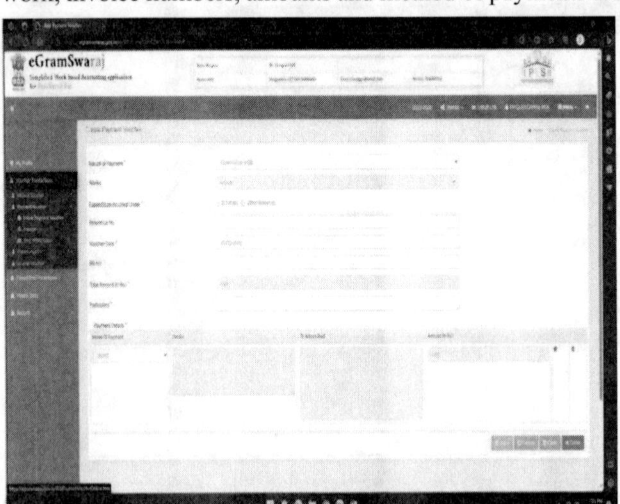

For entering any payment voucher, it is mandatory to select activity in Works Section

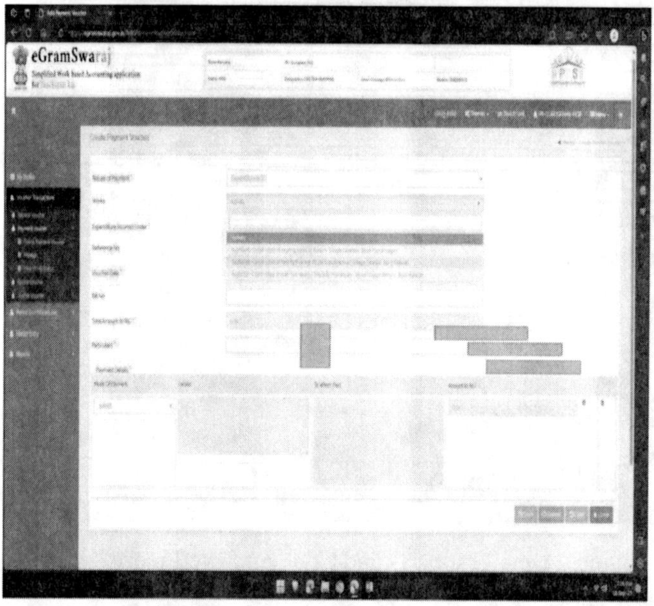

After the works, the Scheme has to be selected

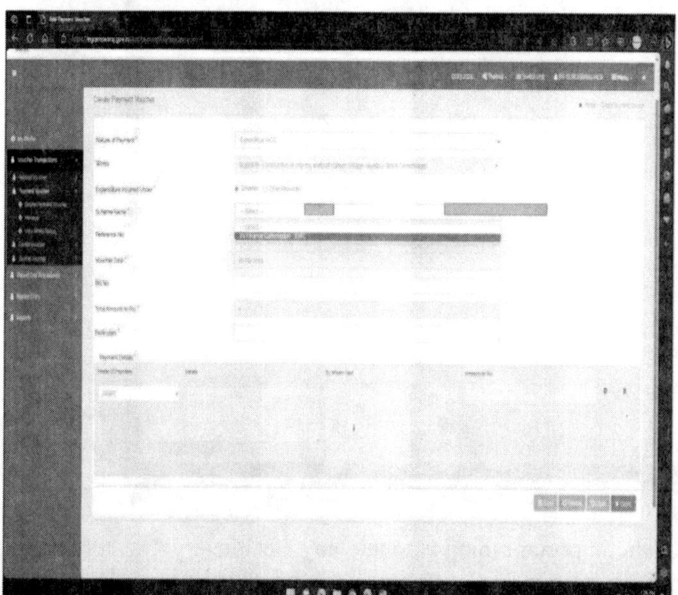

Account Head has to be selected as per classification principles

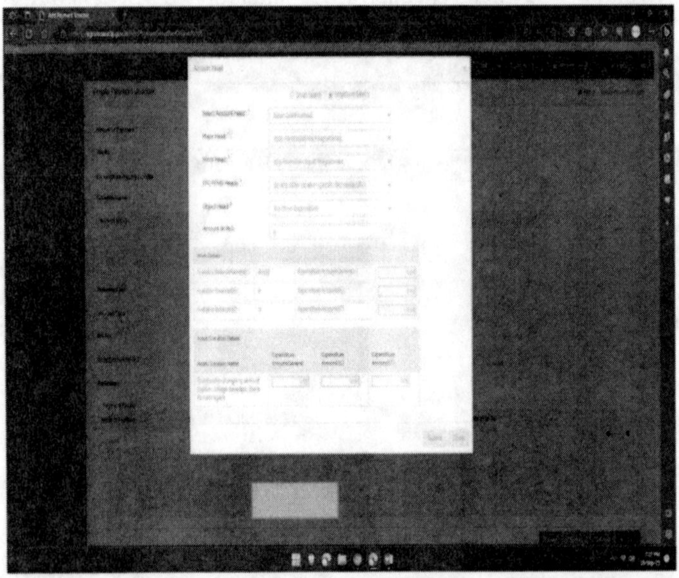

Fill the Payment Detail Properly and Click on Save/Freeze.

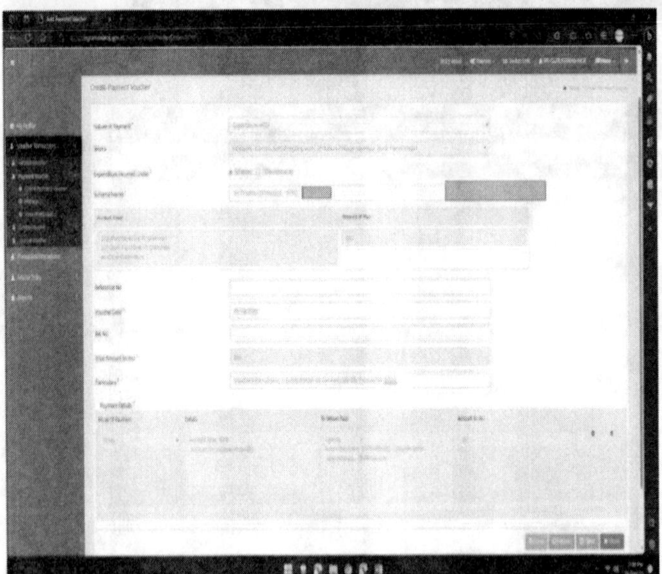

One of the important thing is to add any Beneficiary. It can be done by editing the master entry.

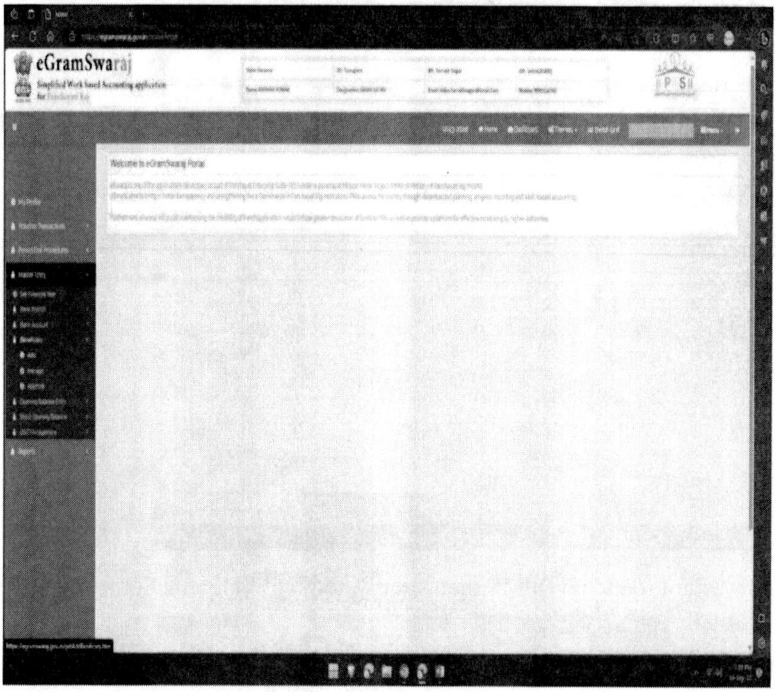

For this, type of beneficiary is to be selected. If required, the beneficiary can be searched by Vender Code are account number.

Select Type of Beneficiary

Search by Account Number or Vendor Code if already exists:

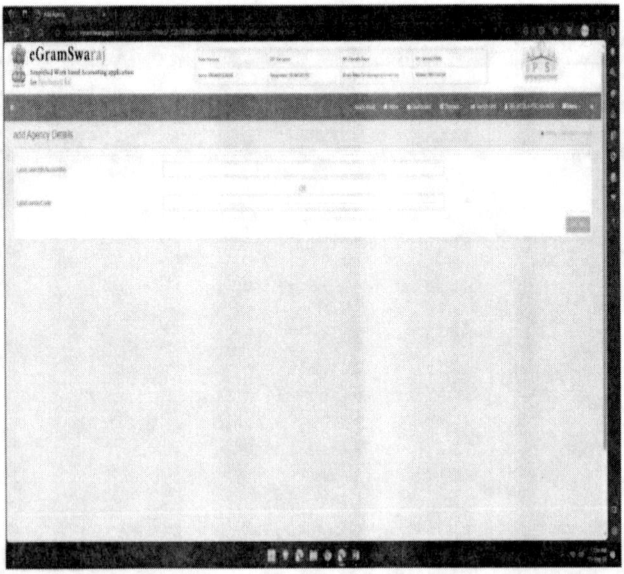

If not found on PFMS then simply add by filling this Form and Save

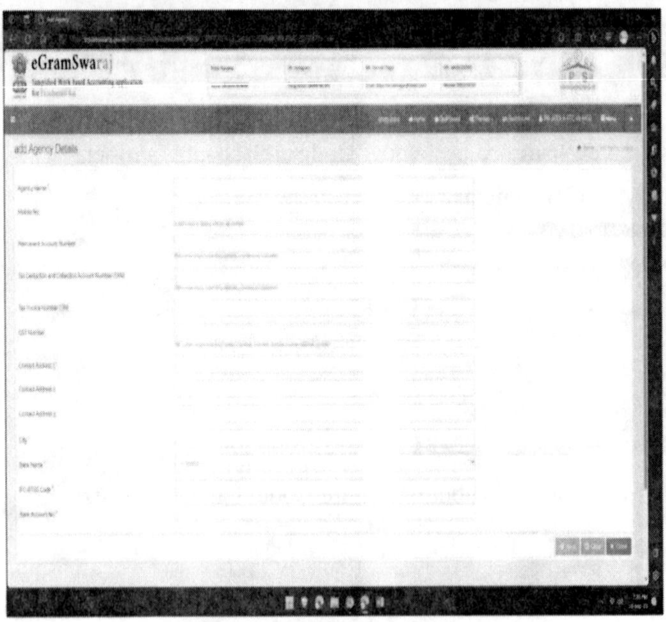

To Close the Day Book, we need to go to:

1. Period End Procedures

2. Closing of Books
3. Scheme-wise Day Book Closure

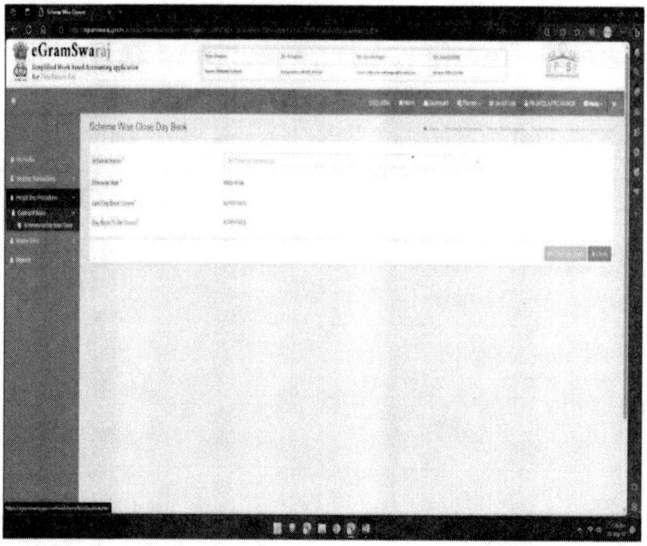

In the ADM User there are many other Options available in the Menu as shown in the figure:

You Can Simply check Fund Detail by Clicking on Fund/Resource Envelope

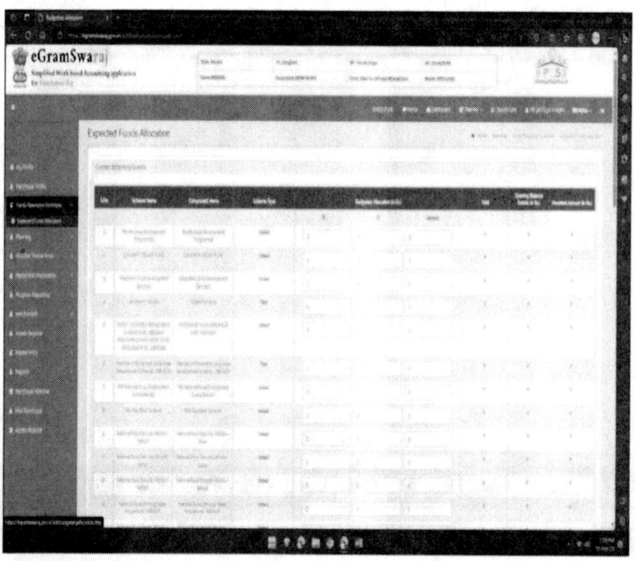

To Add any Activity, we have to go in Planning Section

1. Activity Pool
2. Register Activity

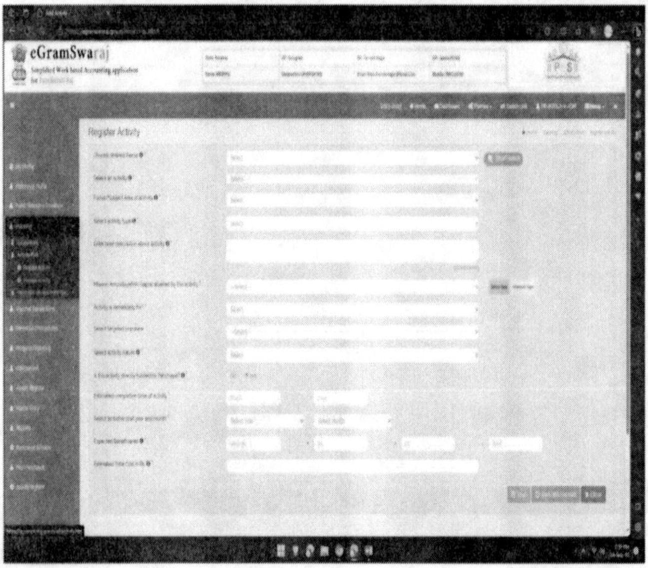

The activity can be uploaded in the Progress Reporting Section.

Period End Procedures Section is used to Close Day/Month/Year book and Bank Reconciliation

The above slides give an overview of entering financial data into the E-gramswaraj portal on a day-to-day basis and also facilitate creating accounting records on Monthly and Yearly basis. It also has an advantage of looking at data from perspectives of schemes, funds or even beneficiaries.

Annexure – I

(para 4 of Chapter 1)

List of 29 subjects as per 73rd Constitutional Amendment

1. Agriculture, including agricultural extension.
2. Land improvement, implementation of land reforms, land consolidation and soil conservation.
3. Minor irrigation, water management and watershed development.
4. Animal husbandry, dairying and poultry.
5. Fisheries.
6. Social forestry and farm forestry.
7. Minor forest produce.
8. Small scale industries, including food processing industries.
9. Khadi, village and cottage industries.
10. Rural housing.
11. Drinking water.
12. Fuel and fodder.
13. Roads, culverts, bridges, ferries, waterways and other means of communication.
14. Rural electrification, including distribution of electricity.
15. Non-conventional energy sources.
16. Poverty alleviation programme.
17. Education, including primary and secondary schools.
18. Technical training and vocational education.
19. Adult and non-formal education.
20. Libraries.
21. Cultural activities.
22. Markets and fairs.

23. Health and sanitation, including hospitals, primary health centres and dispensaries.
24. Family welfare.
25. Women and child development.
26. Social welfare, including welfare of the handicapped and mentally retarded.
27. Welfare of weaker sections, and in particular, of the Scheduled Castes and the Scheduled Tribes.
28. Public distribution system.
29. Maintenance of community assets.

Annexure – II

(para 3.3.1 of chapter 3)

MAJOR HEAD CODES

Sl. No.	Matters listed in schedule XI	Major head classification with code	
1.	Education including primary and secondary schools	2202	General Education
2.	Adult and non-formal education	2202	General Education
3.	Technical training and vocational education	2203	Technical Education
4.	Libraries	2205	Art and Culture
5.	Cultural activities	2205	Art and Culture
6.	Health and sanitation including hospitals, primary health centres and dispensaries	2210	Medical and Public Health
7.	Family Welfare	2211	Family Welfare
8.	Drinking water	2215	Water Supply and Sanitation
9.	Rural housing	2216	Housing
10.	Welfare of weaker sections and in particular the SC and the ST	2225	Welfare of SC, ST and Other Backward Classes
11.	Women and child welfare	2235	Social Security and Welfare
12.	Social welfare including welfare of the handicapped and the mentally retarded	2235	Social Security and Welfare
13.	Agriculture including agricultural extension	2401	Crop Husbandry
14.	Land consolidation and soil conversation	2402	Soil and Water Conservation
15.	Animal husbandry and poultry	2403	Animal Husbandry
16.	Dairying	2404	Diary Development
17.	Fisheries	2405	Fisheries
18.	Social forestry and farm forestry, minor forest produce, fuel and fodder	2406	Forest and Wild Life

Sl. No.	Matters listed in schedule XI	Major head classification with code	
19.	Public distribution system	2408	Food Storage and Warehousing
20.	Programmes like minor irrigation, soil and water conservation, animal husbandry, dairying, afforestation taken up under JGSY, DPAP, DDP, SGSY, EAS, NSAP, IWDP	2501	Special Programmes for Rural Development 43. JGSY 44. DPAP 45. DDP 46. SGSY 47. EAS 48. NSAP 49. IWDP
21.	Land improvement, implementation of land reforms	2506	Land Reforms
22.	Maintenance of community assets	2515	Other Rural Development Programmes
23.	Poverty alleviation programmes	2515	Other Rural Development Programmes (102 – Community Development Roads, Bridges, Culverts Ferries as Sub-heads)
24.	Expenditure on establishment and other miscellaneous activities	2515	Other Rural Development Programme (101 – Panchayati Raj)
25.	Minor irrigation	2702	Minor Irrigation
26.	Rural electrification including distribution of electricity	2801	Power
27.	Non-conventional energy sources	2810	Non-conventional Sources of Energy
28.	Small scale industries including food processing industries	2851	Village and Small Industries
29.	Khadi, village and cottage industries	2851	Village and Small Industries
30.	Roads, culverts, bridges and other means of communication	3054	Roads and Bridges
31.	Expenditure on pensions and other retirement benefits	2071	Pension and Other Retirement Benefits
32.	i. Payment of interest ii. Interest receipts	iii. 2049 iv. 0049	Interest Payments Interest Receipts
33.	Receipts from taxes on income and expenditure	0028	Other Taxes on Income and Expenditure
34.	Land revenue receipts	0029	Land Revenue
35.	Receipts from taxes on motor vehicles and other vehicles	0041	Taxes on Vehicles

Sl. No.	Matters listed in schedule XI	Major head classification with code	
36.	Receipts from taxes on goods and passengers	0042	Taxes on Goods and Passengers
37.	Receipts from taxes and duties on commodities and services	0045	Others Taxes and Duties on Commodities and Services
38.	Receipts on account of public works (non-residential buildings)	0059	Public Works
39.	Pension contributions	0071	Contributions and Recoveries towards Pension and Other Retirement Benefits
40.	Grants from Central Government / State Government for different plan schemes and non-plan grants	1601	Grants-in-aid / Assistance from Central / State Govt.
41.	Receipts on account of compensation and assignments by State Government	1604	Compensation and Assignments from State Government
42.	Loans and advances by the State Government	7601	Loans and Advances by the State Government
43.	Loans and advances to employees	7610	Loans and Advances to Panchayat Employees
44.	Provident Funds	8009	Provident Fund

Annexure – III

(para 3.3.2 of chapter 3)

LIST OF OBJECT HEADS

Sl. No.	Description	Code	Description / Definitions
1.	Salaries	01	Salaries will include pay, allowances in all forms, of personnel. This object classification will also be utilised for recording expenditure on sumptuary allowance.
2.	Wages	02	Wages will include wages of labourers and of staff paid out of contingencies.
3.	Overtime allowance	03	
4.	Pensionary charges	04	Pensionary charges will include contributions to service funds and contributory provident funds in addition to payments of pensions and gratuity in all forms. This will, however, not include social security expenditure such as old age pension.
5.	Honoraria	06	Will include honoraria payable to Chairman and Vice-Chairman of Panchayats, Councilors, Members, Panchayat Secretary.
6.	Domestic travel expenses	11	Domestic travel expenses will cover all expenses on account of travel on duty in India including conveyance and fixed travelling allowance but excluding leave travel concessions. This will also include TA/DA to non-official members on account of travel in India.
7.	Foreign travel expenses	12	Foreign travel expenses will cover all expenses on account of travel on duty outside India. This will also include expenditure on TA/DA to non-official members going on tour abroad.
8.	Office expenses	13	Office expenses will include all contingent expenses for running an office such as furniture, postage, purchase and maintenance of office machines and equipment, liveries, hot and cold weather charges (excluding wages of staff paid from contingencies), telephones, electricity and water charges, stationery, printing of forms, purchase and maintenance of cars and other vehicles for office use as distinct from vehicles for functional purpose like ambulance vans, etc. This will also include petroleum oil and lubricant expenses on vehicles for office use.

Sl. No.	Description	Code	Description / Definitions
9.	Rents, rates, taxes	14	Will include payment of rent for hired buildings, municipal rates and taxes etc. It will also include lease charges for land.
10.	Audit fee	15	
11.	Publications	16	Will include expenditure on printing of codes, manuals and other documents whether priced or unpriced but will exclude expenditure on printing of publicity material. This will also include discount to agents on sale of publications, etc.
12.	Other Administrative Expenses	20	Will include expenditure on canteen hospitality/ entertainment expenses, gifts and expenditure on conducted torus, expenditure on conferences/ seminars/ workshops, etc. and expenditure on other training programmes.
13.	Supplies and materials	21	Will include expenditure on material and supplies, stores and equipment, etc.
14.	Petroleum oil and lubricant	24	Petroleum oil and lubricant will include expenditure on petroleum oil and lubricant for purposes other than those mentioned in Sl. No. 7
15.	Advertising and publicity	26	Advertising and publicity will include commission to agents for sale and printing of publicity material. This would also include expenditure on exhibitions and fairs.
16.	Minor works	27	Will also record expenditure on repairs and maintenance of works, machinery and equipment.
17.	Professional services	28	Professional services will include charges for legal services, consultancy fee, fees to artists, fee for preparation of annual accounts, remuneration to the examiners, invigilators, etc. for conducting examination and all types of remunerations.
18.	Other contractual services	30	Other contractual services will include expenditure on services or commitment charges and notional value of gifts received etc.
19.	Grant-in-aid	31	
20.	Contributions	32	This will also include expenditure on membership of International bodies.
21.	Subsides	33	
22.	Scholarships/stipend	34	
23.	Suspense	43	
24.	Interest	45	Interest will include interest on capital and discount on loans.

Sl. No.	Description	Code	Description / Definitions
25.	Share of taxes/ duties	46	
26.	Other charges	50	Other charges will include payment out of discretionary grants, other discounts, customs duty compensations, awards and prizes, etc. Any other expenditure, which cannot be classified under any of these specified object heads will be debited to this head.
27.	Motor vehicles	51	Motor vehicles include purchase and maintenance of transport vehicles used for functional activities (i.e. ambulance and vans) which are distinct from those used for running and office.
28.	Machinery and equipment	52	Machinery and equipment will include machinery equipment, apparatus, etc. other than those required for the running of an office and special tools and plants acquired for specific works.
29.	Major works	53	Major works will be classified with reference to financial limits as per classification of major works. This will also include cost of acquisition of land and structures.
30.	Investments	54	
31.	Loans and advances	55	Loans and advances will include all loans and advances granted to other Governments, Public Sector Enterprises, undertakings and other Government bodies, etc. but will exclude repayments of borrowings.
32.	Repayments of borrowings	56	
33.	Other capital expenditure	60	
34.	Depreciations	61	
35.	Reserves	62	
36.	Write off/losses	64	Write off/losses will include write off of irrecoverable loans, losses will include trading losses.
37.	Deduct recoveries	70	

Annexure – IV

(Para 4.3.12 of chapter 4)

Exhibit-1

FORM OF ACCOUNTS FOR VARIOUS BOOKS AND REGISTERS

FORM

Cash book of .... Panchayat for the month of ....

Receipts							Disbursements							
Date	Item No.	Particulars of receipts, challans, cheques etc.	Amount (Rs)			Classification	Date	Vr. No.	Particulars	Amount (Rs)				Classification
			Cash	Treasury PLA	Bank					Cash	No. of Cheques	Treasury PLA	Bank	
Total Receipts							Total Disbursement							
To Opening Balance							By Closing Balance							
Grand Total							Grand Total							

Cashier/ Accountant

Officer-in-charge of the Cash Book/ Secretary

Note:

1. Cash book to be closed daily.
2. Denomination detail of physical balance at the end of the day to be indicated.
3. Certificate that 'closing balance' of the cash physically verified and found to tally with the closing balance as per 'cash book' to be recorded by the officer-in-charge/ Secretary at the end of the day.

Exhibit-2

Register of Cheque Books

Panchayat

S. No.	Date of receipt of Cheque-book	Cheque No. from .... to	Initials	To whom issued	Signature of recipient	Date on which Cheque book put to use	Date of receipt of counter folios	Initials	Remarks
(1)	(2)	(3)	(4)	(5)	(6)	(7)	(8)	(9)	(10)

Exhibit-3

Cheque issue Register

..............................Panchayat

S. No.	Date	Payment Voucher No.	Par-ticulars of the vouch-er	Cheque No.	Amount (Rs)	To whom issued	Initials	Date of encash-ment with reference to bank scroll	Remarks
(1)	(2)	(3)	(4)	(5)	(6)	(7)	(8)	(9)	(10)

Monthly Abstract:

1. No. of cheques with details which had remained uncashed at the end of previous month.
2. Of 1 above, No. and details of cheques encashed in this month.
3. No. and details of cheques issued during the month but not cashed.
4. No. and details of cheques remaining uncashed at the end of the month.

Exhibit-4

Register of Contingent Expenditure

Panchayat

Object Heads of Budget												
Date	To whom paid (Budget appropriation for each head)	Number of sub-voucher and contin-gent abstract	Sub-divisions of detailed heads as may be convenient. If the appropriation be not ordinar-ily allotted among the sub-divisions of a detailed head they should be linked by a brace and the amount placed below									

Unusual charges amount	Total of each contingent abstract	Total of each month's bills	Date of detailed bill	Date of ad-mission with initials	Remarks

Exhibit-5

Register of Undisbursed Pay and Allowances etc.

Panchayat

Sl. No.	Bill No. & Date	Net Amount of the Bill		Date of encashment	Total amount remaining undisbursed		Particulars of the amount shown in Col. 5			Dated initials of the func-tionaries	Date of disbursement	Dated initials of the functionaries	Remarks
					Name	Amount							
(1)	(2)	(3)		(4)	(5)		(6)	(7)		(8)	(9)	(10)	(11)
		Rs	P		Rs	P		Rs	P				

Exhibit-6

Demand and Collection Register

Panchayat

Year: ……..20………..to 20……….

Sl. No.	Name and address of the person from whom tax is due	Reference S. No. in the register of assesses	Arrears of past years, if any	Current demand	Remissions, write off and suspen-sion, if any	Total amount due Col. (4+5+6)	Total Amount collected with Date & Receipt No.			Balances at the end of the year (7-8)	Remarks
(1)	(2)	(3)	(4)	(5)	(6)	(7)	(8)			(9)	(10)
							Arrears	Current	Total		

April	May	June	July	August	September	October	November	December	January	February	March	Total
(1)	(2)	(3)	(4)	(5)	(6)	(7)	(8)	(9)	(10)	(11)	(12)	(13)

Exhibit-7

Register of Lands

Panchayat

Sl. No.	Date of transfer, purchase or acquisition	From whom transferred/ acquired	Purpose	Reference to agreement, award, etc.	Area of land	Survey No., etc with boundaries
(1)	(2)	(3)	(4)	(5)	(6)	(7)

Assessment/ Valuation	Boundaries sketch of the land	Building, if any, acquired with the land		Utilization of the build-ing/ land	Amount paid (Rs)	No. and date of voucher	Remarks
		(10)					
(8)	(9)	Brief details of structure	Plinth area	(11)	(12)	(13)	(14)

Exhibit-8

Register of Roads

Panchayat

Sl. No.	Name of Road/ Location	From Village/ Point	To Village/ Point	Length (KM)	Width (Ft.)	Class of Road	Date of Start & of Completion	Total Cost & Average Cost Per (Km) on Construction	Remarks (Details of Repairs with Value)
(1)	(2)	(3)	(4)	(5)	(6)	(7)	(8)	(9)	(10)

Exhibit-9

Register of Immovable Properties other than Lands and Roads

Panchayat

Sl. No.	Date of acquisition, purchase construction or transfer	No. and date of orders underwhich the property was acquired, purchased, constructed/ transferred	Description and situation of property	Purpose for which utilized	Valuation at the beginning of the year	Revaluation, if any, the date and the actual amount on revaluation.	Depreciation at the beginning of the year
(1)	(2)	(3)	(4)	(5)	(6)	(7)	(8)

Depreciation During the Year	Depreciated Value at the end of the year	Response/authority for disposal/ write-off	Whether disposed off amount realised on disposal	Amount realised on disposal	Initials	Remarks
(9)	(10)	(11)	(12)	(13)	(14)	(15)

Exhibit-10

Register of Movable Properties/ Stores

Panchayat

Particulars and description of the property	Authority for purchase & date of purchase	No./ Qty.	Value	No. & Date of the bill in which charged for	Where the property is used or other particulars, if necessary	Date of disposal of property
(1)	(2)	(3)	(4)	(5)	(6)	(7)

Manner of disposal	Qty. disposed off	No. & Date of Order	Cost realised, if sold	Date of Credit into Bank	Balance after each transaction or at the end of each year		Remarks
(8)	(9)	(10)	(11)	(12)	(13)		(14)
					Qty.	Cost	

Exhibit-11

Register of Loans Received

Panchayat

Account of loans of Rs. ……….. received from .... vide order No. .... dated ....

Conditions of Loans

Rate of interest .... per cent to be repaid on ……………. and ....

Principal						Balance after each amount	Interest						Balance	Remarks
Receipts			Payments				Period	Interest due	Total interest due	Interest Paid				
Date	Vr. No.	Amount	Date	Vr. No.	Amount					Date	Vr. No.	Amount		

Exhibit-12

Register of Loans Disbursed

Panchayat

Name of party	Nature of loans	No. and date of sanction	Vr. No. and date of pay-ment	Amount of loan	Interest due	Recoveries in cash or by adjustment					Total recoveries during the year	Balance carried forward	Re-marks
						April		May		….. and so, on			
						Vr. No.	Amount	Vr. No.	Amount	Upto March			

Exhibit-13
Broadsheet of Loans Received/Disbursed

Panchayat

Scheme and loans	Debit				Credit				Total recoveries of loans	Closing balance	Balance as per Plus and Minus memoranda	Remarks
	Opening balance	April	May	And so-on upto March	Opening balance	April	May	And so-on upto March				
Grand Total												

Certified that the balance shown above have been agreed with the Plus and Minus memoranda and with those acknowledged by the Controlling Officer and that the total agrees with the ledger advances.

Exhibit-14
Register of Receipts

Panchayat

Month of Account

Major Head- Taxes on Goods and Passengers

Date	Receipt No./ Reference to Bank Schedule/ Treasury Passbook	Name of Party/ Source	Minor Head-Tolls on Roads, levelled under			Minor Head			Total Amount (Rs)	Abstract for the Day (Rs)
			Taxes on Entry of Goods			Nature of Receipt				
			Octroi							
			Rs	Rs	Rs	Rs	Rs	Rs		

Exhibit-15

Register of Expenditure

(Separate set of Pages for each Major-head)

Panchayat
Month of Account
Major Head

(Amount in Rs.)

Date of Payment	Vr. No.	Amount	Minor Head-I																		Minor Head-II					
			Sub Head-I												Sub Head-II			Total Minor Head-I			Sub Head-I			Sub Head-II		
			Object Head												Object Head				Object Head			Object Head				
			Salaries			Material & Supply			Minor Works			Total Sub-Head														
			P	NP	Total	P	NP	Total	P	NP	Total	P	NP	Total				P	NP	Total						

Exhibit-16

Annual Receipts and Payments Account for Zilla Parishad/Block Panchayat/Village Panchayat Statement of Capital Expenditure during and upto the end of the year.........

Heads of Account- Nature of Expenditure		Expenditure during the year					Expenditure upto the end of the year .... (Progressive) (Rs)
For Example		Non-Plan (Rs)	Plan (Rs)	Centrally Sponsored Schemes (Rs)	State Sponsored Schemes (Rs)	Total (Rs)	
4225	Capital Outlay on Welfare of Scheduled Castes, Scheduled Tribes and Other Backward Classes						
01	Welfare of Scheduled Castes						
277	Education						
282	Health						
283	Housing						
800	Other Expenditure						
02	Welfare of Scheduled Tribes						
277	Education						
282	Health						
283	Housing						
800	Other Expenditure						
03	Welfare of Other Backward Classes						
277	Education						
282	Health						
283	Housing						
800	Other Expenditure						
	Total- 4225						

4515	Capital Outlay on Other Rural development programmes						
800	Other Expenditure						
	Total-4515						
	(Similarly for other capital heads wherever applicable)						
	Grand Total						

Exhibit-17

Annual Receipts and Payments Account for Zilla Parishad/Block Panchayat/Village Panchayat Statement of Receivables & Payables at the end of the year.........

Receivables			**Payables**		
Head of Accounts	**Particulars**	**Amount (Rs)**	**Head of Accounts**	**Particulars**	**Amount (Rs)**
0028	Other Taxes on Income and Expenditure		2049	Interest Payments	
0029	Land Revenue		2059	Public Works	
0035	Taxes on immovable property other than agricultural land		2071	Pension and other retirement benefits	
0041	Taxes on vehicles		2202	General Education	
0042	Taxes on goods and passengers-		2203	Technical education	
0045	Other taxes and duties on commodities and services		2204	Sports and youth services	
	Total Tax Receipts		2210	Medical and public health	
	Non-tax receipts		2215	Water supply and sanitation	
P049	Interest receipts		2216	Housing	
0059	Public Works		2225	Welfare of SC, ST and OBCs	
0202	Education, Sports, Art and culture		2235	Social security and welfare	
0210	Medical and public health		2401	Crop husbandry	

0211	Family welfare		2402	Soil and water conservation	
0215	Water supply and sanitation		2403	Animal Husbandry	
0216	Housing		2406	Forestry and wildlife	
0401	Crop husbandry		2408	Food storage and warehousing	
0405	Fisheries		2501	Special Programmes for rural development	
0406	Forestry and wild life		2505	Rural employment	
0515	Other rural development programmes		2515	Other rural development programmes	
0702	Minor irrigation		2702	Minor irrigation	
0801	Power		2801	Power	
	Total: Non-tax receipts		3054	Roads Bridges	
	Grand Total			Grand Total	

Note:* (1) *The above heads of account are only illustrative. Details may be given as per actual local needs;

(2) Receivables & Payables shown major head-wise above may be further shown minor head, scheme and detail head-wise.

Exhibit-18

Annual Receipts and Payments Account for Zilla Parishad/Block Panchayat/Village Panchayat

Statement of Balances under Deposits and Advances & Loans at the end of the year.........

Head of Account		Opening Balance (Rs)	Receipts (Rs)	Disbursement (Rs)	Closing Balance (Rs)	Details Investments (Rs)
	Deposits					
8443	**Civil Deposits**					
103	Security Deposits					
108	Public Works Deposits					
XX	Deposits by Contractors					
XX	Deposits of earnest money by successful Tenderers in PWD					
124	Unclaimed deposits in GP Fund					
126	Unclaimed deposits in other provident funds					
800	Other deposits					
	Total-8443-Deposits					
8550	**Advances**					
103	**Civil Advances**					
	Other Departmental Advances (each type of Advance to be shown separately)					
	Total-8550-Advances					
	Loans					
6003	**Debt**					
109	**Internal Debt**					
XX	Loans from other Institutions					
XX	Loans from .... (Each Institution to be shown as sub-head)					
800	Loans from Zila Parishad/ Block Panchayat (Programme -wise)					
	Other Loans					
	Total-6003					

Head of Account		Opening Balance (Rs)	Receipts (Rs)	Disbursement (Rs)	Closing Balance (Rs)	Details Investments (Rs)
6004	**Loans and Advances from Central Govt/State Govt**					
01	Non-Plan loans					
800	Other Loans (Details to be given at sub-head level)					
02	Loans for Plan Schemes					
101	Block Loans					
800	Other Loans (Details to be given at sob-head level)					
	Total-6004-Debt					
7610	**Loans to Panchayat employees etc.**					
	(Repayment of loans by employee to be indicated purpose-wise)					
	Total-Loans					
	Grand Total					

Note: (1) The nature of balances, credit or debit may be indicated in the head of account column for opening balance as well as closing balance.

(2) Adverse or minus balances may be explained

Exhibit-19

Annual Receipts & Payments Account for Zilla Parishad/Block Panchayat/Village Panchayat
Statement of Provident Funds etc. and Investments at the end of the year.........

Head of Account		Opening Balance (Rs)	Receipts (Rs)	Disbursement (Rs)	Closing Balance (Rs)	Details Investments (Rs)
8009	**Provident Funds**					
01	Civil					
101	General Provident Fund					
XX	Panchayat Employees Provident Funds					
60	Other Provident Funds					
102	Contributory Provident Pension Fund (each PF to be shown separately)					
	Total-8009-Provident Fund					
8011	**Insurance & Pension Funds**					
107	Employees Group Insurance Scheme					
XX	Insurance Fund					
XX	Savings Fund					
	Total-8011					

Note: *The nature of balances, credit or debit may be indicated under head of account column after the description of the head, for opening balance as well as closing balance.*

Annexure – V

(Para 4.4 of chapter 4)

FORMATS PRESCRIBED BY CAG OF INDIA

MONTHLY/ANNUAL RECEIPTS AND PAYMENTS ACCOUNTS

Format-I

Zilla Panchayat/Panchayat Samiti (Block/Taluk level)/Village Panchayat ………….. for the month/year of………………

RECEIPTS				PAYMENTS							
Opening balance **(i) Cash in hand** **(ii) Balance in bank** **(iii) Balance in Treasury** **(iv) Investments**		**Budget estimates (Rs)**	**Amount Actuals (Rs)**	**HEADS OF ACCOUNT**		**Budget estimates (Rs)**			**Amount Actuals (Rs)**		
HEADS OF ACCOUNT						**Plan**	**Non-Plan**	**Total**	**Plan**	**Non-Plan**	**Total**
PART I – PANCHAYAT FUND				**PART I – PANCHAYAT FUND**							
Revenue Account - ReceiptsTax Receipts				**Revenue Account - Expenditure**							
0028	**Taxes on Profession, Trades etc.**			**2049**	**Interest Payments**						
101	Profession Tax			101	Interest on Provident Fund						
102	Trade Tax			102	Interest on Insurance and Pension Fund						
103	Trade Licence Fees			103	Interest on Other Deposits and Accounts						
901	Share of net proceeds assigned to Panchayats			**2059**	**Maintenance of Community Assets**						
0029	**Land Revenue**			101	Maintenance & Repairs						

101	Land revenue			40	Work Charged Establishment Expenditure						
102	Surcharge on Land Revenue Tax			41	Other Maintenance Expenditure						
103	Taxes on Plantation			102	Furnishing						
901	Share of net proceeds assigned to Panchayats			103	Lease Charges						
0030	**Stamps and Registration Fees**			104	Machinery & Equipments						
101	Duty on Transfer by Sale			**2071**	**Pensions & Other Retirement Benefits**						
901	Share of net proceeds assigned to Panchayats			101	Superannuation & Retirement Allowance						
0035	**Taxes on Property other than Agriculture Land**			102	Commuted value of Pension						
				103	Gratuities						
101	Property Tax on Residential Building			104	Family Pension						
102	Property Tax on Non- Residential Building			105	Leave Encashment Benefit						
901	Share of net proceeds assigned to Panchayats			106	Other Pensionary benefits						
0041	**Taxes on Vehicles**			**2202**	**Education**						
101	Taxes on Cycle/Cart and other receipts from Non-Motor vehicles Act			101	Primary Education						
901	Share of net proceeds assigned to Panchayats			18	Mid-day Meal Scheme						
0042	**Taxes on Goods and Passengers**			19	Sarva Siksha Abhiyan						
101	Toll Tax			102	Secondary Education						
40	Road, Culvert Bridge			103	Adult Education						
41	Ferry			104	Non-formal Education						
42	Water Ways			**2203**	**Technical Training and Vocational Education**						
43	Others			101	Assistance to Universities/ Colleges for Technical Training						
102	Taxes on entry of Goods into Local Area			102	Technical Schools						

103	Taxes on Passengers/ Pilgrims			103	Polytechnic Colleges						
901	Share of net proceeds assigned to Panchayats			104	Vocational Education						
0044	**Service Tax**			**2205**	**Art, Culture and Libraries**						
101	Service Tax			101	Promotion of Art & Culture						
901	Share of net proceeds assigned to Panchayats			102	Public Libraries						
0045	**Taxes on Duties and Commodities**										
101	Entertainment Tax			103	Public Exhibition						
102	Advertisement Tax			104	Sports & Youth Services						
103	Receipts under Education Cess			**2206**	**Market and Fairs**						
104	Receipts under other Acts			101	Market						
105	Forest Development Tax			102	Fairs						
901	Share of net proceeds assigned to Panchayats										
				2210	**Health and Family Welfare**						
				101	Primary Health Centres						
				15	NRHM						
				102	Community Health Centres						
				15	NRHM						
				103	Hospitals & Dispensaries						
				15	NRHM						
				104	Health Sub-Centres						
				15	NRHM						
				105	Other System of Medicine						
				106	Family welfare Services						
Non-Tax Receipts				**2211**	**Women and Child Welfare**						
				101	Women Development Programmes						
0049	**Interest Receipts**			15	NRHM						
101	Interest on Bank Deposit			102	Child Development Programmes						
102	Interest on Loans and Advances			15	NRHM						

800	Other Receipts			**2215**	**Water Supply and Sanitation**						
0059	**Maintenance of Community Assets**			101	Maintenance of Water Supply Line						
101	Rent from Buildings			102	Maintenance and Repair of Tubewells						
102	Recovery of percentage charges			103	Sewerage and Sanitation						
103	Hire Charges of Machineries and Equipments			17	Total Sanitation Campaign						
0071	**Contribution & Recoveries towards Pension and other Retirement Benefits**			**2216**	**Rural Housing**						
				101	House site for Landless						
101	Pension Contribution			14	Indira Awas Yojana (IAY)						
102	Leave and Pension Contribution not levied separately			102	Construction of Houses						
0202	**Education**			14	Indira Awas Yojana (IAY)						
101	Primary Education			103	Maintenance & Repairs of Houses						
102	Secondary Education										
103	Adult Education										
104	Non-formal Education			**2225**	**Welfare of Scheduled Castes, Scheduled Tribes and other Weaker Sections**						
0206	**Market & Fairs**			101	Welfare of Scheduled Caste						
101	Receipts from Markets/Hut			40	Scholarship to Student for Primary Education						
	Receipts from fairs			41	Scholarship to Student for Secondary Education						
				42	Scholarship to Student for Technical Education						
0210	**Health & Family Welfare**			43	Maintenance of SC hostels						
101	Receipts/Contribution from Patients and Others			102	Welfare of Scheduled Tribes						
0215	**Water Supply & Sanitation**			40	Scholarship to Student for Primary Education						
101	Receipts from Water Supply Schemes			41	Scholarship to Student for Secondary Education						

102	Fees, Fines etc			42	Scholarship to Student for Technical Education						
103	Sewerage & Sanitationservices			43	Maintenance of ST hostels						
0216	**Rural Housing**			103	Welfare of other weaker sections						
800	Other Receipts			40	Scholarship to Student for Primary Education						
0403	**Animal Husbandry, Dairying, Poultry and Fuel and Fodder**			41	Scholarship to Student for Secondary Education						
101	Receipts from Cattle and Buffalo Development			42	Scholarship to Student for Technical Education						
102	Receipts from Piggery			43	Maintenance of Weaker Sections' Hostels						
103	Receipts from Poultry Development			**2235**	**Social Security & Welfare**						
104	Receipts from Fodder andFeed Development			101	Social Welfare						
105	Receipts from Other Livestock Development			102	Welfare of Handicapped						
106	Receipts from Milk Supply Scheme			103	Welfare of Mentally Retarded						
0405	**Fisheries**			104	Assistance to Voluntary Organisations						
101	Sale of Fish, Fish Seeds etc			105	Deposit linked Insurance Scheme						
102	Auction of Fishing Rights			**2402**	**Soil and Water Conservation**						
103	Licence Fees, Fines etc			101	Land Improvement						
104	Services and Service Fees			102	Land Reforms						
0406	**Forestry**			103	Land Consolidation						
101	Social forestry			104	Soil and Water Conservation						
40	Sale of Timber & other Forest Produce			**2403**	**Animal Husbandry, Dairying, Poultry and Fuel and Fodder**						
42	Receipts from Forest Plantation			101	Cattle and Buffalo Development						
43	Receipts from Firewood Plantation			102	Piggery Development						
102	Farm Forestry			103	Poultry Development						

40	Sale of Timber & Other Forest Produce			104	Fuel and Fodder Development						
42	Receipts from Forest Plantation			105	Insurance of Livestock and Poultry						
43	Receipts from FirewoodPlantation			106	Dairy Development Projects/ Schemes						
103	Fees			107	Extension & Training						
0435	**Agriculture includingAgriculture Extension**			**2405**	**Fisheries**						
101	Crop Husbandry			101	Processing, Preservation and Marketing						
40	Sale of Seeds			102	Fishery Cooperatives						
41	Receipts from AgricultureFarm			103	Extension & Training						
42	Sale of Manure and Fertilizers			104	Developmental Schemes						
43	Receipts from CommercialCrop			**2406**	**Forestry**						
102	Lease charges for Storage and Warehousing of Agricultural Product			101	Social Forestry						
0515	**Panchayati Raj Programmes**			40	Economic Plantation						
101	District Panchayat			42	Forest Conservation and Development						
40	Licence fee			102	Farm Forestry						
41	Fees for use of Quarry			40	Economic Plantation						
42	Rent for use of Land			42	Forest Conservation and Development						
43	Receipts from Community Development Project			103	Zoological Parks						
44	Other Rates & Fees except Tax Receipts			104	Public Garden						
45	Registration Charges (Other than those not covered under respective functional major heads)			105	Minor Forest Produce						
46	Other Service Fees			**2408**	**Public Distribution System**						
47	Other Fines			101	Procurement & Supply						
102	Panchayat Samiti			102	Assistance to co-operatives						

40	Licence Fee			103	Storage & Warehousing						
41	Fees for use of quarry			26	Maintenance of Warehouses						
42	Rent for use of Land			**2435**	**Agriculture including Agriculture Extension**						
43	Receipts from Community Development Project			101	Crop Husbandry						
44	Other Rates & Fees except Tax Receipts			40	Extension of Farmers Training						
45	Registration charges (Other than those not covered under respective functional major heads)			41	Crop insurance						
46	Other Service Fees			42	Scheme for small marginal farmers and agricultural labourers						
47	Other Fines			43	Horticulture and vegetable crops						
	Gram Panchayat			44	Assistance to farmer cooperation						
				102	Watershed Development Programmes						
40	Licence fee			**2501**	**Poverty Alleviation Programme**						
				101	Central Schemes						
42	Rent for use of Land			11	NREGS						
43	Receipts from Community Development Project			102	State schemes						
45	Registration Charges (Other than those not covered under respective functional major heads)			103	Panchayat Samity schemes						
46	Other Service Fees			104	Gram Panchayat schemes						
47	Other Fines			**2515**	**Panchayati Raj Programmes**						
0702	**Minor Irrigation**			101	District Panchayat Programmes						
101	Receipts from WaterTanks/Ponds			102	Panchayat Samiti Programmes						
102	Receipts from Tubewells			103	Gram Panchayat Programmes						
0801	**Rural Electrification**			**2702**	**Minor Irrigation**						
101	Sale of Power			101	Minor Irrigation Projects						
0810	**Non-Conventional Sourcesof Energy**			102	Water Management						

101	Sale of Bio-Energy										
102	Sale of Solar Energy			**2801**	**Rural Electrification**						
103	Sale of Wind Energy			101	Purchase of Power						
0851	**Village and Small ScaleIndustries**			102	Transmission & Distribution						
101	Handloom Industries			103	Maintenance of Street light						
102	Handicraft Industries			**2810**	**Non-conventional Sources of Energy**						
103	Khadi & Village Industries			101	Maintenance of bio-gas plants						
104	Sericulture Industries			102	Maintenance of Solar Energy Centre						
105	Powerloom Industries			103	Maintenance of Wind Energy Centre						
106	Food Processing Industries			**2851**	**Village and Small Scale Industries**						
107	Other Village Industries			101	Handloom Industries						
	Grants-in-aid			102	Handicraft Industries						
1601	**Grants in aid**			103	Khadi & Village Industries						
101	Grants from Central Government			104	Sericulture Industries						
11	NREGS			105	Powerloom Industries						
12	Sampoorna Gramin Rozgar Yojana (SGRY)			106	Food Processing Industries						
13	Swaranjayanti Gram Swarozgar Yojana (SGSY)			107	Other Village Industries						
14	Indira Awas Yojana (IAY)			**3054**	**Transportation**						
15	National Rural health Mission (NRHM)			101	Roads						
16	Accelerated Rural WaterSupply Programme (ARWSP)			102	Culverts						
17	Total Sanitation Campaign			103	Bridges						
18	Mid Day Meal Scheme			104	Ferries						
19	Sarva Shiksha Abhiyan			105	Waterways						
20	Pradhan Mantri Gram Sadak Yojana			106	Other means of Transportation						
21	Integrated Watershed Management Programme										
22	Integrated ChildDevelopment Services										

103	Grants from other institutions										
Total Revenue Receipts				**Total Revenue Expenditure**							
Capital Account- Receipts				**Capital Account - Expenditure**							
4000	**Capital Receipts**			**4202**	**Capital Outlay on Education**						
800	Other Receipts			101	Construction of Primary Schools						
				102	Construction of Secondary Schools						
				103	Construction of Centre for Adult & Non-formal Education						
				4205	**Capital Outlay on Art, Culture and Libraries**						
				101	Construction of Public Libraries						
				102	Construction of Sports Stadium						
				103	Construction of Training Centre for Art & Culture						
				4206	**Capital Outlay on Market and fairs**						
				101	Construction of permanent structure for Market						
				102	Construction of permanent structure for fairs						
				4210	**Capital Outlay on Health and Family Welfare**						
				101	Primary Health Centres						
				102	Community Health Centres						
				103	Hospitals & Dispensaries						
				104	Health Sub-Centres						
				105	Other system of Medicine						
				4215	**Capital Outlay on Water Supply and Sanitation**						
				101	Laying of Water Supply Line						
				16	ARWSP						
				102	Drilling of Tubewell						
				16	ARWSP						

				103	Sewerage and Sanitation						
				17	Total Sanitation Campaign						
				4216	**Capital Outlay on Rural Housing**						
				101	Purchase of Land						
				14	IAY						
				102	Construction of Houses						
				14	IAY						
				4235	**Capital Outlay on Social Security & Welfare**						
				102	Construction of training centre for welfare of Handicapped						
				103	Construction of Anganwadi Centres						
				4402	**Capital Outlay on Soil & Water Conservation**						
				101	Land Improvement						
				102	Land Reforms						
				103	Land Consolidation						
				104	Soil & Water Conservation						
				4405	**Capital Outlay on Fisheries**						
				104	Construction of Fisheries/Ponds						
				4406	**Capital Outlay on Forestry**						
				103	Development of Zoological Park						
				104	Development of Public Garden						
				4408	**Capital Outlay on Public Distribution System**						
				103	Construction of Godowns & Warehouses						
				4435	**Capital Outlay on Agriculture including Agriculture Extension**						
				101	Construction of Training Centre						
				4515	**Capital Outlay on Panchayati Raj Programmes**						

				101	District Panchayat Programmes						
				102	Panchayat Samiti Programmes						
				103	Gram Panchayat Programmes						
				4702	**Capital Outlay on Minor Irrigation**						
				101	Construction of Works of Minor Irrigation Projects						
				102	Construction Works on Water Management						
				103	Construction Works Watershed Development						
				4801	**Capital Outlay on Rural Electrification**						
				102	Capital outlay on Construction of Sub-Station						
				103	Installation of Street Lights						
				4810	**Capital Outlay on Non-Conventional Sources of Energy**						
				101	Construction of Bio-Gas Plants						
				102	Construction of Solar Energy Centre						
				103	Construction of Wind Energy Centre						
				4851	**Capital Outlay on Village and Small Scale Industries**						
				101	Handloom Industries						
				102	Handicraft Industries						
				103	Khadi & Village Industries						
				104	Sericulture Industries						
				105	Powerloom Industries						
				106	Food Processing Industries						
				107	Other Village Industries						
				5054	**Capital Outlay on Transportation**						
				101	Construction of Village/District Roads						

				20	PMGSY						
				102	Construction of Culverts						
				20	PMGSY						
				103	Acquisition of Land for Construction of Roads/Bridges						
				20	PMGSY						
				104	Construction of Ferry Ghats/ Ferries						
	Total of Part I				**Total of Part I**						

Format of consolidated abstract

Format-II

Consolidated abstract Register of ………………….. for the year of ………………..

(In Rupees)

Head of Accounts	Budget provision		April		May		June		July		August		September		October		November		December		January		February		March		March Supple-mentary		Total	
1	2		3		4		5		6		7		8		9		10		11		12		13		14		15		16	
	P	NP	P	NP	P	NP	P	NP	P	NP	P	NP	P	NP	P	NP	P	NP	P	NP	P	NP	P	NP	P	NP	P	NP	P	NP
Total																														

Format-III

Format of Monthly Reconciliation Statement

Reconciliation Statement of ……………………for the month of …………………

Balance as per Cash Book	With Bank	With Treasury
A. Add (i) Cheques/Cash credited directly into the Bank/Treasury but not taken into the Cash Book (ii) Details of Cheque etc. issued by PRIs but not yet encashed in Bank/ Treasury (iii) Cheque drawn but actually not delivered to the parties (iv) Cheque issued but dishonoured (v) Bank interest not credited into cash book		
B. Deduct (i) Details of Cheques etc. received and entered into Cash Book but not actually deposited into the Bank /Treasury (ii) Cheque received from parties and deposited into bank but dishnoured (iii) Bank charges deducted from bank balance but not taken into Cash Book		
Closing balance as per Cash Book		
Balance as per Bank/Treasury as intimated		
Amount of Difference (if any)		
Details of Difference		

Format of Receivable and Payable

Format-IV

Statement of Receivable and Payable of.......................at the end of the year............

Receivable			Payable		
Heads of Accounts	**Particulars**	**Amount Rs**	**Heads of Accounts**	**Particulars**	**Amount Rs**
Grand Total			Grand Total		

Format-V

Format of Immovable property

Register of Immovable Property of ………………… for the year…………………..

(a) Roads

Sl. No.	Name of Road/ Location	From Village/ Point	To Village/ point	Total Length in K.M.	Average width (feet/m)	Date of construction	Date of repairs	Total cost (in Rupees)	Average cost of construction per K.M	Remarks
1	2	3	4	5	6	7	8	9	10	11

(b) Land

Sl. No.	Date of transfer/ purchaseor acquisition	From whom transferred/ purchased/acquired	Purpose	Reference to agreement, award etc.	Area of land in acres	Survey No. etc with boundaries	Assessment/ Valuation	Whether boundaries sketch of the land is available
1	2	3	4	5	6	7	8	9

Building, if acquired with the land		Utilization of the land/building	Amount paid Rs	No. date and voucher remarks
Brief details ofstructure	Plinth Area			
10		11	12	13

(c) Others

Sl. No.	Date of acquisition, purchase, construction or received or transfer	No. and date of orders under which the property was acquired,purchased, constructed/transferred	Description and location of Assets	Purpose for which acquired	Valuation at the beginning of the year	Revaluation if any, the date and actual amount of revaluation (as per Rules)	Depreciation/ Appreciation as per rules
1	2	3	4	5	6	7	8

Valuation of at the end of the year	If disposed Date of disposal	Reasons for disposal with authority	Amount realised on disposal (in Rupees)	Initials of competent authority	Remarks
9	10	11	12	13	14

Format-VI

Format of Movable property

Register of Movable Property of .... for the year......................

Sl. No.	Date of acquisition, purchase, construction received on transfer	No. and date of orders under which the property was acquired, purchased, constructed/transferred	Description and situation of property	Whether the property is used for any purposes	Valuation at the beginning of the year	Revaluation if any, the date and actual amount of revaluation (as per Rules	Depreciation as per rules
1	2	3	4	5	6	7	8

Valuation of at the end of the year	Whether disposed	Reasons /authority for disposal	Amount realised on disposal	Initials of competent authority	Remarks
9	10	11	12	13	14

Format of Inventory register

Format-VII

Inventory register of .... for the month/year...........................

Description of items

Date	Opening balance		Voucher No. and date	From whom received	Receipts		Total	
	Quantity	Value			Quantity	Value	Quantity	Value
1	2	3	4	5	6	7	8	9

To whom issued and for which purpose	Issued or sold			Closing balance		Signature of the Issuing Officer	Signature of Receiving Officer
	Date	Quantity	Value	Quantity	value		

Format-VIII

Format of Demand, Collection and Balance

Register of Demand, Collection and balance of …………………… for the month/year of .....

Sl. No.	Name and address of the person from whom tax is due	Reference serial No. in the register of assesses	Current-demand	Arrear demand of previous years, if any	Permission/ write off and suspension if any	Total amount due [(4+5)-6]	Total amount collected		
1	2	3	4	5	6	7	8		
							Previous years arrears	Current years	Total